Society of Colonial Wars in the State of Illinois

The Society of Colonial Wars in the State of Illinois

List of Officers and Members

Society of Colonial Wars in the State of Illinois

The Society of Colonial Wars in the State of Illinois
List of Officers and Members

ISBN/EAN: 9783337014414

Printed in Europe, USA, Canada, Australia, Japan

Cover: Foto ©Andreas Hilbeck / pixelio.de

More available books at **www.hansebooks.com**

Society

of

Colonial Wars.

THE

SOCIETY OF COLONIAL WARS

IN THE

STATE OF ILLINOIS.

LIST OF OFFICERS AND MEMBERS.

Together with a record of the service performed by their
Ancestors in the Wars of the Colonies.

PUBLICATION No. 3.

CHICAGO.
1897.

COMPILED BY

THE SECRETARY OF THE SOCIETY.

DAVID OLIPHANT, PRINTER.

OFFICERS, 1897

GOVERNOR

Edward McKinstry Teall
160 La Salle Street

DEPUTY-GOVERNOR

Samuel Eberly Gross

LIEUTENANT-GOVERNOR

Lyman Dresser Hammond

SECRETARY

Seymour Morris
5342 Washington Avenue

DEPUTY-SECRETARY

Scott Jordan

TREASURER

Frank Eugene Spooner
603 Y. M. C. A. Building

REGISTRAR

John Smith Sargent

HISTORIAN

Edward Milton Adams

CHANCELLOR

Judge Frank Baker

CHAPLAIN

Rev. Dr. Frank Wakely Gunsaulus

GENTLEMEN OF THE COUNCIL

Deming Haven Preston
Henry Austin Osborn
Charles Thomson Atkinson
Edward McKinstry Teall
Samuel Eberly Gross
Lyman Dresser Hammond
Frank Eugene Spooner
John Smith Sargent
Edward Milton Adams
Seymour Morris

COMMITTEE ON MEMBERSHIP
Frederick Clifton Pierce
George Butters *
Ebenezer Lane

COMMITTEE ON ENTERTAINMENT
George Samuel Marsh
Hobart C. Chatfield-Taylor
Hiram Holbrook Rose

DELEGATES TO THE GENERAL COURT
Hempstead Washburne
Henry Sherman Boutell
Samuel Eberly Gross
Frank Bassett Tobey
Rev. Abbott Eliot Kittredge, D. D.

ALTERNATES
George Whitfield Newcomb
Albert Eugene Snow
Edward Beecher Case
William Wolcott Strong
Charles Durkee Dana

MEMBERSHIP

MAY 1, 1897.

Edward Milton Adams*
Victor Clifton Alderson
Charles Thomson Atkinson
John Newbury Bagley
Edward Payson Bailey
Judge Frank Baker
Harry Jenkins Bardwell
Warren Lippitt Beckwith
Asahel Frank Bennett
Henry Sherman Boutell
Col. Andrew Sheridan Burt, U. S. A.
George Butters
Edward Beecher Case
Alfred Henry Castle
Chandler Pease Chapman
Charles Cromwell*
Daniel Charles Daggett
Charles Durkee Dana*
Oliver Partridge Dickinson
Alfred Beers Eaton
Marvin Andrus Farr
Charles Newton Fessenden
Albert Judson Fisher
Francis Porter Fisher
Dr. George Foster Fiske
Wyman Kneeland Flint
James Monroe Flower
Henry Clay Fuller
James Harris Gilbert
Edwin Fraser Gillette
Lester Orestes Goddard
Albert Mattoon Graves
Nelson Cowles Gridley
Samuel Eberly Gross*

Rev. Frank Wakely Gunsaulus, D. D.
Lemuel Ruggles Hall
Lyman Dresser Hammond*
Cyrus Austin Hardy
Maj. Forrest Henry Hathaway, U. S. A.
John Whipple Hill
Marvin Allen Ives*
Rev. James Gibson Johnson, D. D.
Scott Jordan*
Rev. Abbott Eliot Kittredge, D. D.
Ebenezer Lane
Joseph Lathrop
John Larkin Lincoln, Jr.
Josiah Lewis Lombard*
John Conant Long
George Mulhollan Lyon
Eames MacVeagh
George Samuel Marsh
Dr. Franklin Adams Meacham
Frederick Laforrest Merrick
William Dorrance Messinger
Charles David Mill
Charles Kingsbury Miller*
Seymour Morris*
George Henry Moore
William John Moore
George Whitfield Newcomb
Henry Austin Osborn
Joseph Edward Otis, Jr.
Philo Adams Otis
Rodman Corse Pell*
Frederick Clifton Pierce
Charles Clarence Poole
Heman Rogers Powers
Deming Haven Preston
Charles Frederick Quincy
Capt. Philip Reade, U. S. A.*
Charles Ridgely
Hiram Holbrook Rose*

Landon Cabell Rose
John Smith Sargent*
Edwin Henry Sedgwick
Frank Slosson
Wyllys King Smith*
Albert Eugene Snow
Frank Eugene Spooner
John Alden Spoor*
William Wolcott Strong
Capt. Eugene L. Swift, U. S. A.
Hobart C. Chatfield-Taylor
Edward McKinstry Teall*
Frank Bassett Tobey
William Ruggles Tucker*
Henry Lathrop Turner
Frederic William Upham*
Gov. William Henry Upham
Henry Sherman Vail
John Demmon Vandercook
Horatio Loomis Wait
Hempstead Washburne*
Samuel Rogers Wells
William Barker Wheelock
Charles Pratt Whitney
Dr. Eugene Wolcott Whitney
William Ward Wight
Frederick Hampden Winston*
Jonathan Edwards Woodbridge
Harry Linn Wright
Walter Channing Wyman

*Life Member.

This Volume is intended to supplement Publication No. 2, which contains the History, Charter and By-Laws of the Illinois Society, together with the Lines of Descent of Members, Nos. 1 to 75.

The Society of Colonial Wars
in the State of Illinois
requests the honor of your presence
at a Banquet, to be given on
Tuesday, December twenty-second, 1896,
at six o'clock,
in commemoration of the
Great Swamp Fight and Forefathers' Day.
The Wellington,
Chicago.

MEMBERS

No. 75 to 109

WITH THEIR LINE OF DESCENT.

JOHN NEWBURY BAGLEY.

DETROIT, MICH.

Tenth in descent from Gov. Thomas Dudley.
Ninth in descent from Gov. Simon Bradstreet.
Ninth in descent from Gov. George Wyllys.
Ninth in descent from Richard Saltonstall.
Eighth in descent from Major John Pynchon.
Eighth in descent from Nathaniel Saltonstall.
Seventh in descent from Col. John Pynchon.
Seventh in descent from Col. Samuel Partridge.
Seventh in descent from Lieut. Joseph Judson.

EDWARD PAYSON BAILEY.

Eighth in descent from William Phelps.
Eighth in descent from Tristram Coffin.
Eighth in descent from Capt. Edmund Greenleaf.
Eighth in descent from Lieut. William Stickney.
Seventh in descent from Lieut. Jonathan Rudd.
Seventh in descent from Samuel Ladd,
Seventh in descent from John Hartshorn.
Seventh in descent from Lieut. Tristram Coffin.
Fifth in descent from Joshua Bayley.
Fourth in descent from Col. Jacob Bayley.

Edward Payson Bailey

ASAHEL FRANK BENNETT.

Seventh in descent from John Prescott, 1st.
Seventh in descent from Thomas Rice.
Seventh in descent from John White.
Sixth in descent from Josiah White.
Sixth in descent from John Prescott, 2d.
Sixth in descent from Thomas Sawyer.
Fifth in descent from John White.
Fifth in descent from John Prescott, 3d.
Fifth in descent from Nathaniel Sawyer.
Fourth in descent from Phineas Sawyer.
Third in descent from Moses Smith, Sr.

COL. ANDREW SHERIDAN BURT, U. S. A.

FORT MISSOULA, MONT.

Sixth in descent from Henry Burt.

C.S. Bret U.S. Army

Alfred N. Castle.

ALFRED HENRY CASTLE.

Seventh in descent from Maj. William Hathorne.
Sixth in descent from John Winchester.
Sixth in descent from Lieut. Thomas Putnam.
Sixth in descent from Lieut. John White.
Fifth in descent from Capt. John Winchester.
Fourth in descent from Maj. General Israel Putnam.

OLIVER PARTRIDGE DICKINSON.

Ninth in descent from Gov. Thomas Dudley.
Eighth in descent from Gov. Thomas Wells.
Eighth in descent from Gov. Simon Bradstreet.
.Eighth in descent from Robert Williams.
Eighth in descent from Hugh Calkin.
Eighth in descent from William Parke.
Seventh in descent from William Hough.
Seventh in descent from Anthony Stoddard.
Seventh in descent from William Douglas.
Seventh in descent from John Leonard.
Seventh in descent from Isaac Williams.
Seventh in descent from John Perkins.
Seventh in descent from Thomas Gridley.
Seventh in descent from John Bissell.
Sixth in descent from Lieut. Daniel White.
Sixth in descent from Benjamin Wait.
Sixth in descent from Col. Samuel Partridge.
Sixth in descent from John Bissell, Jr.
Sixth in descent from Roger Orvis.
Sixth in descent from Joseph Dickinson.
Fifth in descent from Capt. Joseph Hawley.
Fifth in descent from Capt. Daniel White.
Fourth in descent from Col. Oliver Partridge.
Fourth in descent from Capt. Joel White.
Fourth in descent from Capt. Matthew Loomis.

O. B. Dickinson

MARVIN ANDRUS FARR.

Eighth in descent from Surveyor General John Johnson.
Eighth in descent from Capt. John Whipple.
Seventh in descent from John Guild.
Seventh in descent from George Robinson, Jr.
Seventh in descent from John Whitney.
Seventh in descent from Matthias Farnsworth.
Seventh in descent from Hugh Rowe.
Seventh in descent from Capt. John Whipple,
Seventh in descent from John Tower.
Sixth in descent from Capt. John Everett.
Sixth in descent from John Shattuck.
Sixth in descent from Stephen Farr.
Sixth in descent from Simon Stone.
Sixth in descent from Serg. John Randall.

DR. GEORGE FOSTER FISKE.

Fourth in descent from Capt. Martin Severance.

George F. Fiske.

HENRY CLAY FULLER.

Ninth in descent from John Tilley.
Eighth in descent from John Howland.
Eighth in descent from Isaac Allerton.
Eighth in descent from Robert Bodfish.
Eighth in descent from William Crocker.
Eighth in descent from Robert Lee.
Seventh in descent from Ensign John Howland.
Seventh in descent from William Swift.
Seventh in descent from Edmond Goodenow.
Seventh in descent from Thomas Cushman.
Seventh in descent from William Spooner.
Sixth in descent from Nathaniel Warner.
Sixth in descent from James Patterson.
Sixth in descent from John Goodenow.
Fifth in descent from Isaac Cushman.
Fourth in descent from Joseph Patterson.

JAMES HARRIS GILBERT.

Eighth in descent from John Stow, Sr.
Eighth in descent from John Butler.
Eighth in descent from Hezekiah Usher.
Eighth in descent from Thomas Stow.
Seventh in descent from Jonathan Gilbert.
Seventh in descent from John Stow.
Sixth in descent from Lieut. Thomas Stow.
Sixth in descent from Capt. Peter Butler.
Fifth in descent from Lieut. Nathaniel Gilbert.
Fourth in descent from Capt. Nathaniel Gilbert.

Jamie Harris Gilbert

Edwin F. Gillett.

EDWIN FRASER GILLETTE.

Eleventh in descent from William Brewster.
Tenth in descent from Edmund Freeman.
Tenth in descent from Gov. Thomas Prence.
Tenth in descent from Edward Bangs.
Tenth in descent from Richard Sparrow.
Tenth in descent from Francis Cooke.
Ninth in descent from Richard Sears.
Ninth in descent from George Willard.
Ninth in descent from Maj. John Freeman.
Ninth in descent from Capt. Jonathan Sparrow.
Ninth in descent from John Washburn.
Ninth in descent from Experience Mitchell.
Ninth in descent from John Winslow.
Eighth in descent from Capt. Paul Sears.
Eighth in descent from John Washburn, Jr.
Eighth in descent from Lieut. Francis Peabody.
Eighth in descent from Major William Hathorne.
Eighth in descent from Capt. John Capen.
Eighth in descent from Capt. John Appleton.
Seventh in descent from Stephen Mighill.
Seventh in descent from Capt. John Peabody.
Seventh in descent from Lieut. Thomas Putnam.
Sixth in descent from Lieut. Jacob Perley.

ALBERT MATTOON GRAVES.

Eighth in descent from Gov. William Bradford.
Seventh in descent from Lieut. Andrew Newcomb.
Seventh in descent from Maj. William Bradford.
Sixth in descent from Isaac Graves.
Sixth in descent from Richard Goodman.
Fifth in descent from Philip Mattoon.

Albert M. Graves

N. C. Gridley

NELSON COWLES GRIDLEY.

Seventh in descent from Gov. Thomas Welles.
Sixth in descent from Thomas Gridley.

REV. FRANK WAKELY GUNSAULUS, D. D.

Fifth in descent from Stephen Hawley.

John W. Hill

JOHN WHIPPLE HILL.

Eighth in descent from William Bullard.
Seventh in descent from Capt. John Whipple.
Seventh in descent from John Tower.
Seventh in descent from George Barstow.
Seventh in descent from Eleazer Metcalf.
Seventh in descent from Edward Hall.
Seventh in descent from John Read, Sr.
Sixth in descent from Simon Slocomb, Sr.
Sixth in descent from Lieut. Preserved Abel.
Sixth in descent from John Read, Jr.
Fifth in descent from Jeremiah Whipple.
Fifth in descent from Capt. Simon Slocumb.
Fourth in descent from Ebenezer Walker.
Fourth in descent from Ensign John Hall.

MARVIN ALLEN IVES.

Ninth in descent from Rev. Samuel Stone.
Eighth in descent from Ensign Thomas Harris.
Eighth in descent from Capt. Nathaniel Merriman.
Eighth in descent from John Moss.
Eighth in descent from Judge Samuel Lothrop.
Seventh in descent from Samuel Hall.
Fifth in descent from Gideon Ives.

GEORGE MULHOLLAN LYON.

Third in descent from William Lyon.

EAMES MAC VEAGH.

Ninth in descent from Thomas Bunce.
Ninth in descent from Lieut. Samuel Smith.
Ninth in descent from John Bent.
Eighth in descent from John Graves.
Eighth in descent from Dr. Thomas Starr.
Eighth in descent from John How.
Eighth in descent from Thomas Eames.
Eighth in descent from Maj. John Mason.
Seventh in descent from Ensign William Goodrich.
Seventh in descent from Capt. John Waite.
Seventh in descent from Col. Joseph Buckminster.

Eames MacVeagh

Chas. D. Mill

CHARLES DAVID MILL.

KANSAS CITY, MO.

Seventh in descent from Francis Wyman.

GEORGE HENRY MOORE.

Eighth in descent from Capt. Thomas Brooks.
Seventh in descent from Capt. Timothy Wheeler.
Seventh in descent from Capt. John Prescott.
Sixth in descent from Ensign Humphrey Barrett.
Sixth in descent from Capt. James Minott.
Sixth in descent from Capt. Jonathan Prescott.
Sixth in descent from Hon. Peter Bulkley.
Sixth in descent from Simon Lynde.
Sixth in descent from Francis Willoughby.

William John Moore

WILLIAM JOHN MOORE.

Fifth in descent from Alexander Wells.

JOSEPH EDWARD OTIS, Jr.

Ninth in descent from William Thomas.
Eighth in descent from Nathaniel Thomas.
Eighth in descent from Henry Wolcott.
Eighth in descent from Capt. Thomas Miner.
Eighth in descent from Philip Sherman.
Seventh in descent from Dep. Gov. Francis Willoughby.
Seventh in descent from Simon Lynde.
Seventh in descent from Joshua Raymond.
Seventh in descent from Matthew Griswold.
Seventh in descent from John Otis.
Seventh in descent from Nathaniel Thomas.
Seventh in descent from Capt. James Sands.

Joseph E. Otis Jr.

Philo A. Otis.

PHILO ADAMS OTIS.

Ninth in descent from William Thomas.
Eighth in descent from Nathaniel Thomas.
Eighth in descent from Henry Wolcott.
Eighth in descent from Capt. Thomas Miner.
Eighth in descent from Philip Sherman.
Seventh in descent from John Otis.
Seventh in descent from Joshua Raymond.
Seventh in descent from Dep. Gov. Francis Willoughby.
Seventh in descent from Simon Lynde.
Seventh in descent from Matthew Griswold.
Seventh in descent from Nathaniel Thomas.
Seventh in descent from James Sands.

HEMAN ROGERS POWERS.

ST. CHARLES, ILL.

Seventh in descent from Col. Benjamin Church.

Herman R. Powers

Charles Frederick Quincy

CHARLES FREDERICK QUINCY.

Seventh in descent from Lieut. Col. Edmund Quincy.

LANDON CABELL ROSE.

Seventh in descent from Thomas Holbrook.
Sixth in descent from Col. William Fitzhugh,
Fifth in descent from Col. John Henry.
Fifth in descent from Samuel Meredith.
Fourth in descent from Samuel Jordan.

Landow Cabell Rose

E. H. Sedgwick

EDWIN HENRY SEDGWICK.

Eighth in descent from Gen'l Robert Sedgwick.
Seventh in descent from Gov. Wm. Bradford.

FRANK SLOSSON.

KENOSHA, WIS.

Seventh in descent from Capt. James Avery.

Frank Slosson

WYLLYS KING SMITH.

Ninth in descent from John Tilley.
Eighth in descent from John Bigelow.
Eighth in descent from Sergt. John Sheppard.
Eighth in descent from Maj. William Whiting.
Eighth in descent from Gov. John Webster.
Eighth in descent from Richard Treat.
Eighth in descent from John Howland.
Eighth in descent from Nathaniel Dickinson.
Eighth in descent from John Bronson.
Eighth in descent from Samuel Smith.
Eighth in descent from Henry Wolcott.
Eighth in descent from Thomas Coleman.
Seventh in descent from Capt. Richard Bushnell.
Seventh in descent from Capt. Thomas Bull.
Seventh in descent from Jacob Mygatt.
Seventh in descent from Lieut. Robert Webster.
Seventh in descent from Ebenezer Dibble.
Seventh in descent from Capt. John Gorham.
Seventh in descent from Capt. John Miles.
Seventh in descent from John Cooper.
Seventh in descent from Serg. Obadiah Dickinson.
Seventh in descent from Samuel Boardman.
Seventh in descent from Philip Smith.
Seventh in descent from Henry Wolcott, Jr.
Seventh in descent from Maj. Samuel Appleton.
Seventh in descent from Maj. Richard Treat.
Seventh in descent from Ensign William Goodrich.
Sixth in descent from Jabez Gorham.
Sixth in descent from Lieut. Abraham Dickerman.
Fifth in descent from Lieut. Timothy Bigelow.
Fifth in descent from Capt. William Hyde.
Fifth in descent from Capt. Isaac Dickerman.

JOHN ALDEN SPOOR.

Seventh in descent from John Alden.
Seventh in descent from Moses Simmons.

Yours sincerely

E. S. Swift.

CAPT. EUGENE L'HOMMEDIEU SWIFT, U. S. A.

WASHINGTON, D. C.

Seventh in descent from Richard Bourne,

HENRY SHERMAN VAIL.

Seventh in descent from Capt. John Sherman.

H. S. Vail

W. B. Wheelock

WILLIAM BARKER WHEELOCK.

INDIANAPOLIS, IND.

Sixth in descent from Increase Winn.

DR. EUGENE WOLCOTT WHITNEY.

SALT LAKE CITY, UTAH.

Eighth in descent from Henry Wolcott.
Seventh in descent from Major Samuel Appleton.
Sixth in descent from Moses Whitney.

Eugene Wolcott Whitney

ANCESTORS OF MEMBERS.

No. 1 to 109

GEORGE ABBOTT.—(——1689.) Rowley and Andover, a soldier in King Philip's War, February to May, 1675, under command of Maj. Savage, July 24, 1676.

REFERENCE: Bodge's Soldiers of King Philip's War; N E. Hist. and Genealogical Register, Vol. 37, page 375.

64. Harry Jenkins Bardwell.

LIEUT. PRESERVED ABEL.—(——1724.) Served in King Philip's War. Sergeant, 1689; Ensign, 1690. Lieutenant in Capt. Samuel Gallup's Company in Sir William Phipp's expedition against Canada, 1690.

REFERENCE: S. C. W. 1895 Year Book; Savage's Genealogical Dict., Vol. 1., Rehoboth Census of Feb. 7, 1689.

79. John Whipple Hill.

ENSIGN EDWARD ADAMS.—Was Ensign at Medfield, Mass., 1681-1702; Deputy to the General Court many years.

REFERENCE: Society of Colonial Wars Year Book, 1895, p. 191. Tilden's History of Medfield, Mass.

10. Edward Milton Adams.
17. Frederick Clifton Pierce.
51. Franklin Adams Meacham.

JOHN ALDEN.—[1599-1687]—One of the signers of the original "Mayflower Compact." Member under arms of Captain Myles Standish's Duxbury Company, 1643; assistant to all the governors of the Colony, 1633 to 1641, and from 1650 to 1686; representative to the General Court 1641-1649; member of the Council of War 1653-1660 and 1675-1676.

REFERENCE: Society of Colonial Wars Year Book, p. 43. Plymouth Colony Records; Davis Landmarks of Plymouth, p. 4.

4. William Ruggles Tucker.
32. Rev. James Gibson Johnson.
46. George Butters.
53. Edward Beecher Case.
86. John Alden Spoor.

MATTHEW ALLYN.—[——— -1671]—Windsor. Deputy to Massachusetts General Court, 1636; deputy to Connecticut General Court, 1648-1657; assistant, 1658-1667; commissioner for United Colonies, 1660-1664.

REFERENCE: Society of Colonial Wars Year Book, 1895, p. 192.
54. William Ward Wight.

ISAAC ALLERTON.—(1583-1659.) Signer of the Compact on the Mayflower. Deputy Governor, 1621-24.

REFERENCE: Year Book, Society of Colonial Wars, 1896; Allerton Genealogy; Davis Ancient Landmarks of Plymouth.
105. Henry Clay Fuller.

CHRISTOPHER ALMY.—In 1690 he was deputy to the General Court from Portsmouth, R. I., and the same year chosen assistant. Feb. 27, 1690, chosen or elected governor, but refused to serve for reasons satisfactory to the assembly; Aug., 1693, messenger to England from Rhode Island.

REFERENCE: Austin's Genealogical Dictionary of Rhode Island; Church's History.
20. Charles Kingsbury Miller.

CAPT. JOHN APPLETON.—(1622-1699.)   Ipswich, Mass. Lieutenant, 1653; Captain, 1658.

REFERENCE: Society of Colonial Wars Year Book, 1896, p. 277.
90. Edwin Fraser Gillette.

MAJOR SAMUEL APPLETON.—(1624-1696.) Lieutenant, 1668; Captain, 1675; Major and Commander in Chief of Massachusetts Troops, 1675. In command at Springfield, Hatfield and Great Swamp Fight; Sergeant-Major of South Essex Regiment, 1682. Assistant, 1681-6 and '89-92. Imprisoned by Sir Edmond Andros for refusing to pay taxes unjustly levied.

REFERENCE: S. C. W. Register, 1896, pp. 277-278.
87. Dr. Eugene Wolcott Whitney.
93. Wyllys King Smith.

MAJOR-GENERAL HUMPHREY ATHERTON.— [——— 1661]—Deputy from Dorchester to the General Court, 1638, and nine times thereafter; speaker, 1653; assistant, 1654 to 1661; lieutenant, 1645; captain, 1646; commander of the Ancient and Honorable Artillery Company, 1650; commanded expedition against Pesacus, a Narragansett chief, 1650; major-general, 1661.

REFERENCE: Savage's Genealogical Dictionary of New England. Society of Colonial Wars Year Book, 1895, p. 194.
6. Lyman Dresser Hammond.

CAPTAIN JAMES AVERY.—Commanded "100 dragoons" raised near New London, 1673, to fight against Indians; was commander of a company of 40 whites, besides about 100 friendly Indians at the Swamp fight, 1675; was one of the captors of Canonchet, 1676; was twelve times deputy to legislature, 1658-1680.

REFERENCE: Savage's Genealogical Dictionary; Conn. Colonial Records.

10. Edward Milton Adams.
51. Franklin Adams Meacham.
92. Frank Slosson.

LIEUTENANT WILLIAM AVERY.—[1622-1687]—Dedham, Mass.; physician; member of Ancient and Honorable Artillery Company in 1654; representative to the General Court for Springfield, 1669; lieutenant of Dedham Military Company, 1673.

REFERENCE: Society of Colonial Wars Year Book; Savage's Genealogical Dictionary; Whitman's History of Ancient and Honorable Artillery Co., p. 164; Dedham, Mass., Town Records; Lane family, p. 17.

45. Francis Porter Fisher.
68. Albert Judson Fisher.
70. Charles Ridgely.

ENSIGN JOHN BAGG.—[1665-1740]—For many years sergeant of the military company of Springfield, Mass., and its Ensign in 1738.

REFERENCE: N. E. Hist. and Gen. Register, Vol. 29, p. 293; "West Springfield Centennial," p. 109; History of Springfield by M. A. Greene, p. 220.

68. Albert Judson Fisher.

THOMAS BAKER.—[1618-1700]—Ensign of East Hampton, (Conn.) Company, 1654; assistant, 1658-1663.

REFERENCE: Palfrey's New England, Vol. 2, p. 635; East Hampton Records, Vol. 1, p. 58.

25. Frank Baker.

REV. THOMAS BALCH.—Of South Dedham, Mass. A. B. Harvard College, 1733; was chaplain in the Louisburg expedition in 1744.

REFERENCES: See Life and Journal of Dr. Manasseh Cutler, p. 18.

57. Charles Clarence Poole.

SERGEANT JOHN BALDWIN.—Sergeant of Milford (Conn.) Militia, 1658.

REFERENCE: New Haven Historical Collection, p. 263-7.

25. Frank Baker.

EDWARD BANGS.—[1592-1678]—Of Plymouth and East-
ham, Mass.; overseer or captain of the Guard against the
Indians; a member of the Plymouth Military Company, 1643.
General Court, 1692.

REFERENCE: N. E. Hist. and Gen. Register, Vol. 8, p. 368;
Pierce's Colonial Lists, p. 76.

18. Scott Jordan.
32. Rev. James Gibson Johnson.
37. Frank Bassett Tobey.
61. Victor Clifton Alderson.
90. Edwin Fraser Gillette.

JONATHAN BANGS.—Of Eastham, Mass., was constable,
1672; selectman, 1674-1676, and later; was Ensign at Eastham,
1680, and also Ensign again, appointed Oct. 2, 1689.

REFERENCE: Plymouth Colonial Records, Vol. 5, p. 167; Vol. 6,
p. 40, 218.

32. Rev. James Gibson Johnson.
50. Albert Eugene Snow.

CAPTAIN GEORGE BARBOUR.—Of Dedham and Medfield,
Mass. Was a member of the Ancient and Honorable Artillery
Co., 1646, was chief military officer of Medfield after 1649;
defended Medfield in King Philip's War, 1675-6, and fought
against the Indians at Seekonk and Rehoboth, 1676.

REFERENCE: Tilden's Medfield, 312, 87, 90; N. E. Hist. and
Gen. Reg., Vol. 1, 184.

54. William Ward Wight.

LIEUT. EBENEZER BARDWELL, JR.—Of Hatfield,
Mass., a member of Ephraim Williams' Company on Dec. 19,
1747; Ensign in Capt. John Ball's Company at Ft. William
Henry, Oct. 11, 1756; Second Lieutenant in Capt. John Burke's
Company; enlisted March 21, 1759; served until Nov. 30, 1759;
Lieutenant Captain Moses Porter's Company in expedition to
Crown Point.

REFERENCE: Mass. Archives, Vol. 96, p. 40.

64. Harry Jenkins Bardwell.

LIEUTENANT PEREZ BARDWELL.—Of Hatfield, Mass.,
a member of Capt. William Shepard's Company, June 24 to
Dec. 4, 1761; a member of Capt. Salah Barnard's Company, enlisted March 5, 1760, until Oct. 5, promoted to Corporal Oct. 6,
serving until Nov. 30, 1760.

REFERENCE: Mass. Archives, Vols. 96, p. 40; 99, p. 131.

64. Harry Jenkins Bardwell.

SERGEANT ROBERT BARDWELL.—Robert Bardwell was a private or trooper under Lieut. Phineas Upham; was made Sergeant and given command of the Hadley and Hatfield garrisons, leading them in the "Falls Fight."

REFERENCE: Mass. Archives, Vol. 68, p. 212; Vol. 114, p. 610.

64. Harry Jenkins Bardwell.

DEPUTY-GOVERNOR JAMES BARKER.—(1623-1702.) Deputy-Governor of Rhode Island Colony 1678; Assistant and Deputy, 1663-86; Corporal, 1644; Ensign, 1648.

REFERENCE: S. C. W. Year Book, 1896, p. 281.

75. Warren Lippitt Beckwith.

CORPORAL THOMAS BARNARD.—Of Salisbury and Amesbury, Mass., was a soldier in King Philip's War, 1675-77; a corporal in Capt. Wm. Turner's troop of Dorchester, Boston and Charlestown.

REFERENCE: Bodge's Soldiers in King Philip's War, p. 193-205; Mass. Archives, Vol. 68, p. 228; Savage's, Vol. 1, p. 120; N. E. H. and G. R., Vol. 6, p. 207.

2. Captain Philip Reade.

ENSIGN HUMPHREY BARRETT.—(1630-1716.) Ensign of the Concord, Mass., Company in 1688; Deputy to the General Court in 1691.

REFERENCE: Mass. Colonial Records; Potter's Concord Genealogies; Soc. Col. Year Book, 1895, p. 195.

81. George Henry Moore.

GEORGE BARSTOW.—(1614-1654.) Cambridge. Member of the "Ancient and Honorable Artillery Company of Massachusetts" in 1644.

REFERENCES: History of the Ancient and Honorable Artillery Co., 1637 to 1738, by Oliver Ayer Roberts, Vol. 1, pp. 136-137-138; Savage's Gen. Dict.; Records of Plymouth Colony; Dedham Records; Deane's History of Scituate.

79. John Whipple Hill.

WILLIAM BARTHOLOMEW.—(1640——.) Lieutenant of the Massachusetts Bay Colonial forces. Participated in defense of Hatfield, King Philip's War, September 19, 1677.

REFERENCE: Massachusetts Bay Court Records, Vol. 6, p. 104.

47. Major Forrest Henry Hathaway, U. S. A.

ROBERT BARTLETT.—[1603-1676].—Served in Capt. Myles Standish Company, 1632.

REFERENCE: Society of Colonial Wars Year Book, 1895, p. 196; Pierce's Colonial Lists.

39. George Samuel Marsh.
61. Victor Clifton Alderson.

ELISHA BASSETT.—Was captain at Sandwich, Mass. He held commission under Royal Governors Shirley, Pownal, Dudley and Hutchinson.

REFERENCE: Freeman's History of Cape Cod, Vol. 1, p. 335.

37. Frank Bassett Tobey.

WILLIAM BASSETT.—Was member of Capt. Myles Standish's Military Company at Duxbury, Mass., Aug., 1643.

REFERENCE: Pierce's Colonial Lists, p. 76.

37. Frank Bassett Tobey.

WILLIAM BASSETT, JR.—Was a member of Capt. Myles Standish's Military Company at Duxbury, Mass., Aug., 1643.

REFERENCE: Pierce's Colonial Lists.
37. Frank Bassett Tobey.

WILLIAM BASSETT.—Was Chief Marshal of Plymouth Colony, 1689 to 1692; was also captain at Sandwich, Mass. Representative.

REFERENCE: Pierce's Colonial Lists, p. 5; Plymouth Colonial Records, Vol. 6, p. 205, 1670-1721. Society of Colonial Wars Year Book, 1895.
37. Frank Bassett Tobey.

JOHN BATES.—[1642-1716]—Of Chelmsford. A soldier in Capt. Thomas Wheeler's Company, King Philip's War, 1675-6; also in Chelmsford Garrison, 1691-2.

REFERENCE: N. E. Hist. and Gen. Reg., Vol. 38, p. 40; Vol. 43, p. 264 and 373.
18. Scott Jordan.

JOHN BATES, SR.—Was appointed Ensign of train band at Stamford, Conn., Oct., 1685; was deputy to General Court, 1689-90.

REFERENCE: Connecticut Colonial Records, Vol. 2, p. 183; Vol. 4, p. 3.
10. Edward Milton Adams.

SAMUEL BATES.—Was appointed lieutenant of 2d Company or Train Band at Stamford, Conn., May, 1730.

REFERENCE: Connecticut Colonial Records, p. 274.
10. Edward Milton Adams.

LIEUT. COLONEL JACOB BAYLEY.—(1726-1815.) Newbury, Mass.; Hamstead, N. H., and Newbury, Vt. Lieutenant in Capt. Allcock's Company, in Col. Peter Gilman's Regiment, September 22 to December 14, 1755. Captain of the Second Company in Col. Nathaniel Meserves' Regiment, March 5 to November 5, 1758. Lieutenant Colonel in Col. John Goffes' Regiment, serving at Crown Point from March to November, 1760.

REFERENCE: N. H. State Archives.
88. Edward Payson Bailey.

JOSHUA BAYLEY.—(1685——.) A member of Capt. Hugh March's Second Foot Company of Newbury, Mass., January 15, 1710-11.

REFERENCE: N. E. Hist. and G. Register, Vol. 30, p. 434.
88. Edward Payson Bailey.

THOMAS BAYLEY.—(1652-1675.) Weymouth. A soldier in King Philip's War under Capt. Lathrop; was slain at Bloody Brook, September 18, 1675.

REFERENCE: Savage, Vol. 1, p. 108.
64. Harry Jenkins Bardwell.

ELNATHAN BEACH.—Was commissioned Ensign at Wallingford, Conn., Oct., 1733; lieutenant, Oct., 1740; captain, Oct., 1741.

REFERENCE: Connecticut Colonial Records, Vol. 1726-1735, p. 474; Vol. 1735-1743, p. 342-418.
59. Charles Pratt Whitney.

AUSTIN BEARSE.—A member of the Barnstable Military Company in Plymouth Colony in August, 1643.

REFERENCE: Pierce's Colonial Lists, p. 73.
24. Lemuel Ruggles Hall.

SAMUEL BENNETT.—[1665-1742]—Lancaster and Shrewsbury, Mass. Soldier in Queen Anne's War at Lancaster in 1704, in the garrison commanded by Ensign Peter Josslin. Was commander of garrison in 1711.

REFERENCE: Marvin's "History of Lancaster, Mass.," p. 110; Mass. Archives, Vol. 71, p. 876.
68. Albert Judson Fisher.

SAMUEL BENNETT.—[——1684]—Of Providence and East Greenwich, R. I.; in 1652 chosen general sergeant. In 1655, freeman. Oct. 27, 1656, he was ordered paid £20 for his services as sergeant; 1668-74-78, deputy to the General Court.

REFERENCE: Austin's Genealogical Dictionary of Rhode Island.

39. George Samuel Marsh.

SAMUEL (2) BENNETT.—Of East Greenwich and Coventry, R. I.; 1685, a freeman. In 1690 deputy to the General Court and a Lieutenant.

REFERENCE: Austin's Genealogical Dictionary of Rhode Island.
39. George Samuel Marsh.

GEORGE BENNIT.—Killed by Indians in the Lancaster, Mass., massacre, led by Monaco, "One-eyed John," Sunday, Aug. 22, 1675, during King Philip's War.

REFERENCE: Nourse's "Early Records of Lancaster, Mass.," p. 30, 98, 99, 252, 306, 314, 320; Marvin's "History of Lancaster, Mass.," p. 61-101.
68. Albert Judson Fisher.

DANIEL BELDEN.—(1648-1731.) Hatfield and Deerfield, Mass. His wife and three children were killed by the Indians during King Philip's War, September 16, 1696, and he with his two children were captured and taken to Canada. Returned 1698. His second wife was captured and killed by the Indians during Queen Anne's War. Appointed upon the Committee of Fortification in said war with Col. Partridge et al.

REFERENCE: Sheldon's Deerfield, Vol. 1, p. 254-256-288-304; Vol. 2, p. 80.
48. Henry Austin Osborn.
64. Harry Jenkins Bardwell.

JOHN BENT, SR.—(1596-1672.) Sudbury. Private in Maj. Simon Willard's Troop of Horse expedition against Ninigret, 1654, Colony of Massachusetts Bay.

REFERENCES: S. C. Wars, Year Book 1896, p. 284; N. E. H. & G. Register, Vol. 48, p. 288.
99. Eames Mac Veagh.

JOHN BIGELOW.—[1617-1703]—Watertown, Mass. Soldier in the Pequot War and in King Philip's War. His son, John, Jr., was taken captive by the Indians at Lancaster, Oct. 15, 1705.

REFERENCE: Society of Colonial Wars Year Book; Hudson's "History of Marlborough," p. 325; Hudson's "Annals of Sudbury, Wayland and Maynard," p. 232, Ed., 1891; Bond's "Watertown," p. 29; N. E. Hist. and Gen. Register.

68. Albert Judson Fisher.
93. Wyllys King Smith.

LIEUT. TIMOTHY BIGELOW.—(1702-1747.) Appointed Adjutant in army at Cape Breton, March 4, 1745, in place of Cyprian Nicols, and was Second Lieutenant May, 1746, in company that went in Canadian Expedition.

REFERENCE: Colonial Records of Conn., Vol. 9, p. 93.

93. Wyllys King Smith.

EBENEZER BILLINGS.—Of Stonington, Conn., was Ensign, Oct. 12, 1721; Lieutenant, Oct. 14, 1731, in Colonial forces.

REFERENCE: Connecticut Colonial Records, 1717-25, p. 275; 1726-1731, p. 349.

10. Edward Milton Adams.
51. Franklin Adams Meacham.

HON. JAMES BISHOP.—Secretary of New Haven Colony, 1661-1665; assistant, Conn. Colony, 1668-83; deputy governor, 1683-91.

REFERENCE: Colonial Wars Year Book, 1894; Savage's Genealogical Dictionary.

42. Charles Thomson Atkinson.
48. Henry Austin Osborn.

JOHN BISSELL.—(——-1677.) Deputy General Court, Connecticut, 1648, '50, '52, '53. One of a troop of 30 horse, the first in the Colony, organized by the General Court and placed under command of Capt. John Mason, 1657-8. Soldier in King Philip's War.

REFERENCES: Conn. Col. Records, Vol. 1, pp. 174-211-231-246-309; Stiles' History of Ancient Windsor, Vol. 1, pp. 177-221; Hinman's First Settlers of Conn.

96. Oliver Partridge Dickinson.

JOHN BISSELL, JR.—(——1693.) Soldier in King Philip's War. Quartermaster of County Troop of Hartford, Conn., 1677; Cornet of the Troop, 1681.

REFERENCES: Conn. Col. Records, Vol. 2, p. 311; Vol. 3, p. 91; Stiles' Hist. of Ancient Windsor, Vol. 1, p. 221; Hinman's First Settlers of Conn.

96. Oliver Partridge Dickinson.

CAPTAIN OZIAS BISSELL.—Served during six years in the French and Indian War. Was in an engagement on Lake George in 1755. Was taken prisoner to Havana in 1762, where he was imprisoned for nearly nine months.

REFERENCE: Stiles History Ancient Windsor, Vol. 2, p. 1ʳ3.

8.   George Francis Bissell.

WILLIAM BLAKE.—[—— 1663]—Of Dorchester, Mass.; a member of the Ancient and Honorable Artillery Company of Boston.

REFERENCE: Savage's Genealogical Dictionary.

4.   William Ruggles Tucker.

MATTHEW BLANSHAN.—Early settler and land patentee at Esopus (near present Kingston) N. Y. His daughter, Katherine DuBois, wife of Louis, with her three children, another daughter, Maria Chrispel and her child, and his two younger children, were all carried into captivity at the Indian attack upon the village, June 7, 1663. He joined a rescuing expedition led by Louis Du Bois, which defeated the savages and recovered most of the captives. Member of the Hurley Military Company commanded by Capt. Paulding, stationed at Marbleton, Muster Roll dated April 4, 1670.

REFERENCE: Brodhead's History of New York, Vol. 2, p. 311-312; New York Historical Documents (Colonial Archives), Vol. 13, p. 246, 448, 449.

13.   Samuel Eberly Gross.

THOMAS BLISS.—Was in King Philip's War in 1675, and his name appears in the list of those who drew Cedar Swamp lots for service performed in said war.

REFERENCE: Bodge's Soldiers in King Philip's War, pp. 443-5.

70.   Charles Ridgely.

THOMAS BLODGETT.—Of Woburn, Mass., was private in the West Middlesex Regt. of Mass. Bay Troops; was in the garrison having headquarters at Chelmsford, his rendezvous being the garrison house of John Spaulding on March 6, 1692.

REFERENCE: N. E. Hist. and Gen. Reg., Vol. 43, p. 374.

62.   William Dorrance Messinger.

SAMUEL BOARDMAN.—(1615-1673.) Assistant Colony of Connecticut.

REFERENCE: S. C. W. Register, 1895, p. 200.

93.   Wyllys King Smith.

ROBERT BODFISH.—A member of Lieut. John Blackmer's Company at Sandwich, Mass., in August, 1643.

REFERENCE: Pierce's Colonial List, p. 73.
105. Henry Clay Fuller.

RICHARD BOURNE.—Was a member of Council of War for town of Sandwich, Mass., Feb. 29, 1675.

REFERENCE: Pierce's Colonial Lists, p. 98.
4. William Ruggles Tucker.
37. Frank Bassett Tobey.
103. Capt. Eugene L. Swift, U. S. A.

JOHN BOUTELL.—Was one of the soldiers in the Reading, Mass. Co. in the Narragansett War. A private in Captain Joseph Gardiner's Company.

REFERENCE: New England Historical and Genealogical Register, Vol. 39, p. 175-177.
14. Henry Sherman Boutell.

LIEUTENANT HENRY BOWEN.—[1633-1723]—Of Roxbury, Mass., and Woodstock, Conn., under Captain Isaac Johnson in Great Swamp fight.

REFERENCE: Society of Colonial Wars Year Book, 1894, p. 39; N. E. H. and G. Register, Vol. 39, pp. 74-78.
1. Seymour Morris.

GOVERNOR WILLIAM BRADFORD.—[1589-1657]—Governor of Plymouth Colony, 1621, 1632, 1637, 1639-1643, 1648-1656. Came over in Mayflower, and was one of the signers of the Compact.

REFERENCE: Savage's Genealogical Dictionary; Plymouth Colony Records; Society of Colonial Wars Year Book, 1894; Davis' Ancient Landmarks of Plymouth.
4. William Ruggles Tucker.
21. William Wolcott Strong.
38. George Whitfield Newcomb.
40. Chandler Pease Chapman.
64. Harry Jenkins Bardwell.
89. Albert Mattoon Graves.
109. Edwin Henry Sedgwick.

MAJOR WILLIAM BRADFORD.—[1624-1704]—Commanded the expedition for relief of Swanzey, June 28, 1675. Wounded by Indians in "Ye Greate Swamp Fight" Dec. 19, 1675. Deputy Governor of Plymouth, 1682-1686.

REFERENCE—Palfrey's History of New England, Vol. 2, p. 131, 148, 387, 408; Year Book, Society of Colonial Wars, 1894; Davis' Ancient Landmarks of Plymouth; Savage.

4. William Ruggles Tucker.
21. William Wolcott Strong.
38. George Whitfield Newcomb.
40. Chandler Pease Chapman.
64. Harry Jenkins Bardwell.
89. Albert Mattoon Graves.

GOV. SIMON BRADSTREET.—Governor of Massachusetts Bay Colony, 1679 to 1686, and 1689 to 1692.

REFERENCES: Mass. Col. Records; Dudley Genealogy; N. E. H. & G. Register, Vol. 1, p. 75.

57. Charles Clarence Poole.
101. John Newbury Bagley.
96. Oliver Partridge Dickinson.

GEORGE BRAMHALL.—Killed by the Indians in the fight at Falmouth, Me., Sept. 21, 1689.

REFERENCE: History of Portland, p. 284; Davis' Landmarks of Plymouth, p. 40.

46. George Butters.

LOVE BREWSTER.—A member of the Duxbury, Mass., Military Company in August, 1643.

REFERENCE: Pierce's Colonial Lists, p. 76.

61. Victor Clifton Alderson.

ELDER WILLIAM BREWSTER.—(1566-1644.) Drafted in the cabin of the "Mayflower" the first written constitution, called the "Mayflower Compact." A member of the Plymouth Company under Capt. Myles Standish in August, 1643.

REFERENCES: Pierce's Colonial Lists, p. 76; S. C. W. 1895 Year Book, p. 203; Plymouth Col. Records.

61. Victor Clifton Alderson.
90. Edwin Fraser Gillette.

JOHN BRONSON.—[—— 1680]—Of Hartford, Conn.; deputy to the General Court; soldier in the Pequot battle of 1637. Took part in the Fort fight.

REFERENCE: Society of Colonial Wars Year Book, 1894, p. 47.

1. Seymour Morris.
43. Harry Linn Wright.
64. Harry Jenkins Bardwell.
93. Wyllys King Smith.

CAPTAIN THOMAS BROOKS.—[—— 1667]—Concord, Mass.; deputy to the General Court seven times, 1642-1660; Captain Concord Militia.

REFERENCE: Society of Colonial Wars Year Book, 1894.
25. Frank Baker.
81. George Henry Moore.

COL. JOSEPH BUCKMINSTER.—(1666-1747.) Framingham, Mass. Commanded Company of Grenadiers in Sir Charles Hobby's expedition. Deputy to Colony of Massachusetts Bay, 1709-1723.

REFERENCES: Barry's History of Framingham, Mass., p. 300; S. C. War Year Book, p. 292.
99. Eames Mac Veagh.

REVEREND GERSHOM BULKELEY, M. D.—[1636-1713] —Was Chaplain and Surgeon to the Connecticut Troops in King Philip's War.

REFERENCE: Society of Colonial Wars Year Book, 1895, p. 205, appendix page 17.
7. Edward McKinstry Teall.

HON. PETER BULKELEY (1643-1688) of Concord, Mass.; Deputy four terms; Speaker of the House, 1676; Governor's Assistant, 1676-1685.

REFERENCES: Colonial Records, Mass. Bay Colony; General Society Year Book, 1895, p. 292.
81. George Henry Moore.

CAPT. THOMAS BULL.—(1605-1684.) Hartford, Conn. A Lieutenant in the Pequot War and Captain of the troops at Saybrook Fort during the Andros tyranny.

REFERENCES: S. C. W. 1895, p. 205; Hinman's Conn. Settlers, pp. 386-7-8; Trumbull's Hist. of Conn., Vol. 1, pp. 328-330.
93. Wyllys King Smith.

WILLIAM BULLARD.—(1594-1687.) Dedham. Member of Capt. Lusher's Train Band, Dedham, 1648.

REFERENCE: Mass. Archives, Vol. 67, p. 43.
79. John Whipple Hill.

THOMAS BUNCE.—A soldier in the Pequot war.
REFERENCE: S. C. Wars, 1896 Year Book, p. 293.
99. Eames Mac Veagh.

THOMAS BURGESS.—A private in the Sandwich, Mass. Company, 1643.

REFERENCE: Pierce's Colonial Lists, p. 73.
32. Rev. James Gibson Johnson.

THOMAS BURNHAM.—[1617-1688]—Soldier in King Philip's War.

REFERENCE: Stiles History of Windsor, Vol. 1, p. 227.
21. William Wolcott Strong.

BENJAMIN BURT.—(1680-1759.) Northampton. Taken captive with his wife by the Indians after the battle of Deerfield Meadows, Queen Anne's War, February 29, 1704. Both were released in 1706 by an expedition under Ensign Sheldon.

REFERENCE: Sheldon's Deerfield I., 304-308-333-355.
64. Harry Jenkins Bardwell.

HENRY BURT.—Of Dorchester and Springfield, Mass. Member of the first Military Company of Springfield. In 1657 he was clerk of the Train Band.

REFERENCE: Mass. Bay Colonial Records, Vol. 4, part 1, p. 314; Savage's Genealogical Dictionary.
39. George Samuel Marsh.
64. Harry Jenkins Bardwell.
68. Albert Judson Fisher.
76. Col. Andrew Sheridan Burt.

JONATHAN BURT.—At the time of the burning of Springfield, Mass., by the Indians, Oct. 5, 1675, during King Philip's War, was one of those who defended the town.

REFERENCE: Longmeadow Centennial, p. 305, appendix, p. 7; Morris' Historic Address, "The Burning of Springfield," p. 35; Mason A. Greene's History of Springfield; Geo. Bliss' Address in Chapin Family History, p. 280.
68. Albert Judson Fisher.

JOSEPH BURT.—[1673-1759]—A member of the force in garrison at Northfield in Capt. Joseph Kellogg's Co. from Nov. 20, 1723, to May 20, 1724; also in the Crown Point Expedition.

REFERENCE: N. E. Hist. and G. R.
39. George Samuel Marsh.

CAPT. RICHARD BUSHNELL.—(1652-1727.) Of Norwich, Conn. 1693, Ensign of Norwich Train Band; 1698, Lieutenant of Norwich Train Band; 1701, Captain of Norwich Train Band; Representative for 37 session from 1691——; Town Clerk, 1691-'95, 1698, 1702-1727; 1717-18, Commissioner in the Indian and Mason controversy.

REFERENCES: Caulkins' Hist. of Norwich, p. 84; Bodge's Soldiers in King Philip's War, pp. 441-444.

71. Ebenezer Lane.
93. Wyllys King Smith.

JOHN BUTLER.—Roxbury, Mass. A member of the Ancient and Honorable Artillery Company of Boston in 1644.

REFERENCE: Whitman's History of the Ancient and Honorable Artillery Co., p. 143.

77. James Harris Gilbert.

CAPT. PETER BUTLER.—(——1699.) Of Boston, Mass., and Middletown, Conn. A Captain in the Local Militia.

REFERENCE: Savage's Genealogical Dictionary, Vol. 1.

78. James Harris Gilbert.

WILLIAM BUTTER.—Of Woburn, Mass. Private in Captain Joseph Eyll's Company at capture of 300 Indians at Cecheco (Dover), Sept. 4, 1676.

REFERENCE: N. E. Hist. and Gen. Register, Vol. 41, p. 409; Savage's Genealogical Dictionary; Sewell's History of Woburn.

46. George Butters.

CAPTAIN DAVID CADY.—[1703]—Of Killingly, Conn. Oct., 1747, was commissioned captain of the 1st Company or Train Band of Killingly.

REFERENCE: Connecticut Colonial Record, Vol. 9, p. 320.

18. Scott Jordan.

CAPTAIN DAVID CADY, JR.—[1742-1807]—May, 1774, commissioned Ensign of the 12th Company or Train Band of the 11th Conn. Regiment; May, 1774, Captain of the 4th Company, 11th Regiment; Captain of the 9th Company, 21st Regiment, March, 1775.

REFERENCE: Colonial Records of Connecticut, Vol. 14, p. 268, 290, 398.

18. Scott Jordan.

CAPTAIN JOSEPH CADY.—[1666-1742]—Of Groton, Mass., and Killingly, Conn. In garrison at Groton, Mass., 1791-2. Commissioned Lieutenant of the Train Band, Killingly, Conn., Oct., 1708; commissioned Captain of the Train Band of Killingly, May, 1721; was the first Captain of the town of Killingly; Deputy to General Assembly from Killingly, 1731-33-34 and 1739.

REFERENCE: N. E. Hist. and Gen. Reg., Vol. 43, p. 373; Connecticut Colonial Records, Vol. 5, p. 75; Vol. 6, p. 239.

18. Scott Jordan.

NICHOLAS CADY.—Of Watertown and Groton. A member of Capt. Mason's Watertown Train Band, 1653.

REFERENCE: N. E. Hist. and Gen. Reg., Vol. 34, p. 281.

18. Scott Jordan.

HUGH CALKIN.—[1600-1690]—Gloucester and Lynn, Mass., and New London and Norwich, Conn. Town Clerk and Representative to the General Court for Gloucester, 1650-1651. Representative for Norwich, 1663-64. Representative for New London, 1665, and after. Was appointed Commissioner for enlisting men for an expedition against the Indians on May 21, 1653; and on Oct. 3, 1654.

REFERENCE: Savage's Gen. Dict. of N. E.; Year Book Society of Colonial Wars, 1895; Mass. Bay Colonial Records, Vol. 2, p. 9°; Vol. 4, part 1, pp. 2 and 54; Colonial Records of Connecticut, Vol. 1; Vol. 2, p. 91; Bavson's History of Gloucester, p. 51 to 67; Caulkin's History of New London, pp. 84, 85 and 158.

68. Albert Judson Fisher.
96. Oliver Partridge Dickinson.

CAPT. JOHN CAPEN.—(1613-1692.) Member A. & H. Artillery Co.; 1646, Deputy from Worcester, Mass.; 1671, 1673, 1678, Captain of Militia.

REFERENCE: Society of Colonial Wars Year Book, 1896, p. 296.

90. Edwin Fraser Gillette.

RICHARD CARDER.—Of Boston, Mass., Portsmouth and Warwick, R. I., May 25, 1636, was a freeman; March 7, 1638, he was one of 19 signers of the compact of Portsmouth; 1659-60-63, he was Commissioner. In 1664 to 1666 he was Deputy to General Court. In 1666 he was chosen Assistant, but refused.

REFERENCE: Austin's Genealogical Dictionary of Rhode Island.

39. George Samuel Marsh.
75. Warren Lippitt Beckwith.

WILLIAM CARPENTER—Of Providence, R. I., was Deputy in 1664-5, 1675, 1676 and 1679; Assistant to the Governor, 1665 to 1672.

REFERENCE: Austin's Genealogical Dictionary, p. 37; Society of Colonial Wars Year Book, 1895, p. 207.

39. George Samuel Marsh.

CAPTAIN JOHN CARTER.—[1616-1692]—Of Woburn, Mass.; Ensign, 1651; Lieutenant, 1664; Captain, 1672; Captain of Woburn Company in King Philip's War.

REFERENCE: Year Book of the Society of Colonial Wars.

1. Seymour Morris.
28. Cyrus Austin Hardy.

JOSIAH CHAPIN.—Was captain of Mass. Colonial forces at Mendon; Sergeant, 1685; Ensign, 1687; Lieutenant, 1689, and captain, 1692; was representative many years.

REFERENCE: Annals of Mendon (Metcalf) pp. 98, 104, 106, 108, 114, 126; Mass. Archives, Vol. 107, p. 161; Vol. 70, p. 296-97.

10. Edward Milton Adams.
49. Frank Eugene Spooner.
51. Franklin Adams Meacham.

DEACON SAMUEL CHAPIN.—Springfield, Mass. For many years was appointed with John Pynchon and Eleazer Holyoke by the General Court of Mass. Bay Colony to administer the government of Springfield. At the burning of Springfield, Oct. 5, 1675, during King Philip's War, he was a participant in repelling the attacking Indians from the fortified houses.

REFERENCE: History of Springfield, p. 19 and 35, by Morris; Mass. Col. Records, Vol. 4, part 1, p. 115, 136, 213, 214, 379; History of Springfield by Mason A. Greene, p. 100, 124, 162, 578; Savage's Gen. Dictionary American Ancestry, Vol. 7; Chapin Family, p 239; Morris' Historic Address, "The Burning of Springfield," p. 35.

68. Albert Judson Fisher.
40. Chandler Pease Chapman.

SETH CHAPIN.—(Son of Josiah). Was captain of Mass. Colonial forces at Mendon, 1714, and later; was representative many years.

REFERENCE: Annals of Mendon (Metcalf), p. 169-208.

10. Edward Milton Adams.
49. Frank Eugene Spooner.
51. Franklin Adams Meacham.

LIEUTENANT JOHN CHATFIELD.—Was commissioned ensign in Parish of Oxford, Conn., Oct., 1743; was commissioned Lieutenant of second company Derby, Oct., 1750.

REFERENCE: Connecticut Colonial Records; Vol. 8, p. 566; Vol. 9, p. 554.

52.   Hobart Chatfield Chatfield-Taylor.

DEACON FRANCIS CHICKERING.—(——1658.) Of Dedham, Mass. A member of the Ancient and Honorable Artillery Company of Boston in 1649.

REFERENCES: History of the Ancient and Honorable Artillery Co., by O. A. Roberts, 1896, pp. 125-129; Fiske Genealogy, by Pierce, 1896, p. 50; N. E. H. and G. Register, Vol. 9, p. 346.

7.   Edward McKinstry Teall.

COL. BENJAMIN CHURCH.—(1639-1718.) Of Duxbury, Mass., and Little Compton, R. I. July 7, 1682, he was commissioned Magistrate. In 1682-3-4, Deputy to the General Court of Plymouth Colony. He was a Captain and Colonel of the Colonial forces and one of the capturers of the Indian chief King Philip.

REFERENCE: S. C. W. 1895 Year Book, p. 210.

85.   Heman Rogers Powers.   •

CAPTAIN DANIEL CLARK.—[1622-1710]—Secretary of Colony, 1658-64, and 1665-6. Lieutenant of first body of cavalry in Connecticut, 1658; Captain of same troop in 1664; in 1666 appointed by the General Court with Governor Winthrop to call out the militia and commissioned officers in case of the invasion of the enemy of the colony, 1658-66.

REFERENCE: Ancient Windsor, Vol. 1, p. 125; Vol. 2, p. 153; Salisbury, Vol. 3, p. 230.

21.   William Wolcott Strong.
42.   Charles Thomson Atkinson.
71.   Ebenezer Lane.

CAPT. JOHN CLARK.—Of Saybrook, Conn., who had the rank of a Major of a Foot Company in an expedition against Canada.

REFERENCE: Caulkin's Hist. of New England, p. 381.

56.   Wyman Kneeland Flint.

JOHN CLARKE.—Was one of the corporation named in the charter of Connecticut granted by King Charles II. He was deputy to the General Court twenty-one sessions. Commissioner for Saybrook in 1664; was a soldier in the great battle of Pequot Indians of Mystic in 1637.

REFERENCE: Colonial Records of Connecticut, Vol. 1, p. 3, Vol. 2, p. 13; Society of Colonial Wars Year Book, 1895, p. 211.

70.   Charles Ridgely.

AARON CLEVELAND.—Of Woburn, Mass. Was in Capt. John Cutler's Co. which was engaged in Sudbury, Lancaster, Marlborough and vicinity during King Philip's War.

REFERENCE: N. E. Hist. and Gen. Reg., Vol. 42, p. 299.
10. Edward Milton Adams.
51. Franklin Adams Meacham.

JOSIAH CLEVELAND.—[1667-1709]—Of Woburn and Chelmsford, Mass., and Canterbury, Conn. Served as a private in the Indian War, 1688-9; also in the garrison in the West Regiment of Middlesex, 1691-2.

REFERENCE: Cleveland Genealogy; New England Historical and Genealogical Register, Vol. 43, p. 373; Savage's Genealogical Dictionary, Vol. 2, p. 406; Sewall's History of Woburn, Mass., p. 601; Society of Colonial Wars Year Book, 1895, p. 211.
18. Scott Jordan.

CAPTAIN JOSIAH CLEVELAND.—[1713-1793]—Of Canterbury, Conn., May, 1759, was commissioned captain of the 9th Company or Train Band of the 11th Connecticut Regiment.

REFERENCE: Colonial Records of Connecticut, Vol. 11, p. 267.
18. Scott Jordan

MOSES CLEVELAND.—[1624-1701-2]—Of Woburn. Was a member of the militia company in 1676. Was also in garrison at Chelmsford, Mass., Nov. 20, 1675, and was a soldier in King Philip's War.

REFERENCE: New England Historical and Genealogical Register, Vol. 43, pp. 261 and 279.
10. Edward Milton Adams.
18. Scott Jordan.
51. Franklin Adams Meacham.

ROBERT COATES.—Of Lynn, Mass., was under Capt. Turner at Hadley, Mass., constituting one of the garrison at that place from April 6, 1676, to Aug. 24, 1676, and later.

REFERENCE: Mass. Archives, Vol. 68, p. 212; N. E. Hist. and Gen. Reg., Vol. 41, p. 29; Vol. 43, p. 264; Society of Colonial Wars Year Book, 1894, p. 95.
10. Edward Milton Adams.

CORPORAL EDWARD COBURN.—[1618 ——]—Was a soldier in the local military company at Chelmsford during King Philip's War, 1676, also during the French and Indian War, 1689. Was in command of Coburn's Garrison on the east side of the Merrimac River.

REFERENCE: Savage's Gen. Dict., Vol. 1, p. 423.
2. Captain Philip Reade.

TRISTRAM COFFIN.—(1609-1681.) Of Newbury, Mass. Commissioner at Salisbury, 1655. Chief Magistrate for Nantucket under Gov. Lovelace, N. Y.

REFERENCE: Soc. Colonial Wars Year Book, p. 302.
88. Edward Payson Bailey.

LIEUT. TRISTRAM COFFIN.—(1632-1704.) Of Newbury, Mass. Lieutenant at Newbury, 1683. Deputy to General Court, 1695, 1700-02, Colony of Massachusetts Bay.

REFERENCES: Society of Colonial Wars Year Book, 1896, p. 303; History of Newbury, Mass.
88. Edward Payson Bailey.

DANIEL COLE.—Member of Yarmouth Military Company, 1643.

REFERENCE: Pierce's Colonial Lists, p. 74.
58. Frederick Laforrest Merrick.

THOMAS COLEMAN.—(1600-1674.) In 1654 appointed to procure men and necessaries for expedition against Ninnigret in Narragansett War.

REFERENCE: S. C. W. Register 1895, p. 212.
93. Wyllys King Smith.

WILLIAM COLLIER.—[—— 1670]—Was Governor's Assistant twenty-eight years, from 1634 to 1665, Plymouth Colony; was Commissioner to the United Colonies, 1643. Representative Plymouth Colony, was member of the Colonial "Council of War," Sept. 27, 1642 and later.

REFERENCE: Pierce's Colonial Lists, p. 4-85; Plymouth Colony Records, 1633-1670; Society of Colonial Wars Year Book, 1895; Savage's Gen. Dictionary, Vol. 1, p. 433.
10. Edward Milton Adams.
15. Josiah Lewis Lombard.
50. Albert Eugene Snow.
51. Franklin Adams Meacham.
61. Victor Clifton Alderson.
63. Rev. Abbott Eliot Kittredge.

GEORGE COLTON.—[—— 1699]—Of Longmeadow, Mass., Quartermaster.

REFERENCE: N. E. Hist. and Gen. Register, Vol. 33, p. 202.
40. Chandler Pease Chapman.
42. Chas. Thomson Atkinson.

LOT CONANT, JR.—Of Beverly, Mass., was soldier in Capt. Joseph Gardiner's Company in King Philip's War, 1675-6, at the Great Swamp fight.

REFERENCE: Society of Colonial Wars Year Book, 1895, p. 212; Savage's Gen. Dictionary.

17. Frederick Clifton Pierce.

ROGER CONANT.—Was Governor of the Massachusetts Colony at Cape Ann, 1625-6, and at Salem, 1627-9. Deputy later.

REFERENCE: Society of Colonial Wars Year Book, 1895, p. 212; Savage's Gen. Dictionary.

17. ' Frederick Clifton Pierce.
60. John Conant Long.

LIEUTENANT JAMES CONVERSE.—[1620-1715]—Of Charlestown and Woburn, Mass. Lieutenant of Woburn Company in Garrison in King Philip's War; Deputy, 1679.

REFERENCE: Year Book, Society of Colonial Wars.

1. Seymour Morris.
28. Cyrus Austin Hardy.

MAJOR JAMES CONVERSE.—[1645-1705]—Of Woburn, Mass. Deputy to the General Court five times, 1679, 1680, 1683-1686, 1689, 1691, 1693; Speaker, 1699, 1702-3; Commander in defense of Storer's Garrison, 1691-1692, for which service he was made Major.

REFERENCE: Year Book, Society of Colonial Wars, p. 185-188; "Magnalia Christi Americana," by Rev. Cotton Mather, p. 613-18; Morris Genealogy, p. 38 to 50; Woburn Records of Births, Marriages and Deaths.

1. Seymour Morris.
28. Cyrus Austin Hardy.

CAPTAIN JOSIAH CONVERSE.—[1684]—Woburn, Leicester and Brookfield, Mass. Representative to the General Court, 1715. Captain of the Woburn Company.

REFERENCE: Year Book of the Society of Colonial Wars, 1894; Sewell's History of Woburn, Mass.; History of Leicester, Mass.

1. Seymour Morris.

LIEUTENANT JOSIAH CONVERSE.—[1710-1775]—Of Woburn and Leicester, Mass., and Stafford, Conn.; Representative to the General Court, 1733, from Leicester; Lieutenant of the Leicester Company.

REFERENCE: Year Book of Society of Colonial Wars, 1894; History of Leicester, Mass.

1. Seymour Morris.

MAJOR   AARON   COOK.—[1610-1690]—Westfield,   Mass.
Deputy to General Court, 1668; Ensign, 1676; Captain of Garrison in King Philip's War; Major of Hartford Troops, 1687.

REFERENCE: Ancient Windsor, Vol. 2, p. 160; Colonial Wars Year Book, 1895.

   42. Charles Thomson Atkinson.
   43. Harry Linn Wright.
   45. Francis Porter Fisher.
   64. Harry Jenkins Bardwell.

CAPTAIN   AARON   COOK.—[1641-1716]—Ensign,   1663;
Captain, 1678-1713, Hadley Militia. Deputy, 1689-91-93-97.

REFERENCE: Society of Colonial Wars Year Book, 1895, p. 213.

   42. Charles Thomson Atkinson.
   43. Harry Linn Wright.
   45. Francis Porter Fisher.
   64. Harry Jenkins Bardwell.

MOSES COOK.—Killed in King Philip's War, Westfield,
1676.

REFERENCE: Savage's Genealogical Dictionary, N. E., p. 418; Ancient Windsor.

   42. Charles Thomson Atkinson.

SAMUEL COOK.—Was commissioned Lieutenant at Wallingford, Conn., Oct., 1741. He was promoted Captain, Oct.,
1742.

REFERENCE: Connecticut Colonial Records, Vol. 1735-1743, p. 418-488.

   59. Charles Pratt Whitney.

THADDEUS COOK.—Was commissioned Ensign of Second
Company of Preston, Conn., in Eighth Conn. Regiment in Oct.,
1755. Lieutenant in Troop of Horse, Tenth Conn. Regiment in
Oct., 1757; Captain of Second Company or train band at Preston, Conn., in May, 1763; Captain of troop of horse in Tenth
Conn. Regiment in May, 1764. He was Deputy from Wallingford, Conn., to the General Court, 1775.

REFERENCE: Connecticut Colonial Records, Vol. 1751-1757, p. 414; Vol. 1757-1762, p. 69; Vol. 1762-1767, p. 142-355; Vol. 1775-1776, p. 2-91; Vol. 1776, p. 29

   59. Charles Pratt Whitney.

FRANCIS COOKE.—[1583-1663]—Came over in the Mayflower. Served in expedition against Indians, under Capt.
Myles Standish, February 16, 1621. Member of the Plymouth
Military Company, June 22, 1644.

REFERENCE: Society of Colonial Wars Year Book, 1895, p. 213.

   34. Hempstead Washburne.
   72. Lester Orestes Goddard.
   90. Edwin Fraser Gillette.

JOHN COOPER.—(——1689.) First settler New Haven, and signed the fundamental agreement there in 1639. Deputy a number of times and Assistant in 1676.

REFERENCE: Hinman's First Puritan Settlers, p. 706.

93. Wyllys King Smith.

LIEUTENANT THOMAS COOPER.—[1619-1675]—Of Springfield, Mass. Lieutenant of the Springfield Company. When the Indians attacked Brookfield, Mass., August 7, 1675, Lieut. Cooper commanded the rescuing force of twenty-seven dragoons and the Springfield Indians; was in command at Springfield, Mass., and was killed by the Indians at the burning of that town on Oct. 5, 1675; in 1668 was representative to the General Court of Massachusetts Bay Colony.

REFERENCE: Records of Society of Colonial Wars; Hubbard's "History of Western Massachusetts," and "History of New England;" "Massachusetts Bay Colonial Records;" History of Springfield, Mass.; History of North Brookfield, Mass.; History of Hadley, Mass.

68. Albert Judson Fisher.

WILLIAM CROCKER.—A member of Lieut. Thos. Dimmock's Company of Barnstable, Mass., in August, 1643.

REFERENCE: Pierce's Colonial Lists, p. 73.

105. Henry Clay Fuller.

WILLIAM CROMWELL.—A member of the Legislative Council of Lord Proprietor of Maryland, Lord Baltimore. He was paid forty pounds of tobacco by the Assembly of Maryland in November, 1678, for services rendered in an expedition against the Nanticoke Indians in the same year.

REFERENCE: Archives of Maryland Records, 1678-1683, p. 96: Genealogy of Chenoweth and Cromwell Families; History of Virginia, p. 341.

11. Charles Cromwell.

JAMES CUDWORTH.—[—— 1682]—Was representative, 1649-56-59; Assistant, 1656-8; Captain of Militia; commanded in early part of King Philip's War the whole force of Plymouth Colony; Deputy Governor in 1681.

REFERENCE: Savage's Genealogical Dictionary.

24. Lemuel Ruggles Hall.

JOHN CUNNABELL.—[1649-50 ——]—Was member of the company of Capt. William Turner, for services in King Philip's War. The company defended Northampton against the Indians, March 14, 1676, and defeated the Indians at the battle of "Great Falls," May 18, 1676. (For his services under Capt. Turner he received £3 8s 6d, as per journal of John Hull, who was treasurer of Massachusetts Colony, 1675-1680.)

REFERENCE: New England Historical and Gen. Register; Newcomb Genealogy; Cunnabell Genealogy.

38.   George Whitfield Newcomb.

LIEUT. PHILIP CURTIS.—Lieutenant in Capt. Henchman's Company; slain by the Indians in an expedition which left Boston in 1675 for the rescue of some captives taken by the savages at the Town of Marlborough. The captives were recovered, but in an assault at the Indian camp at Hassanomossett (now Grafton) led by Lieut. Curtis, he was killed.

REFERENCE: Bodge's Soldiers in King Philip's War.

56.   Wyman Kneeland Flint.

ISAAC CUSHMAN.—(1676-1727.) Lieutenant of Militia company, Plympton, Mass., for many years.

REFERENCE: Cushman Genealogy.

105.   Henry Clay Fuller.

THOMAS CUSHMAN.—A member of the Plymouth, Mass., Military Company in August, 1643.

REFERENCE: Pierce's Colonial List, p. 76.

105.   Henry Clay Fuller.

ENSIGN JAMES CUTLER.—[1606-1694]—Soldier in King Philip's War.

REFERENCE: Year Book 1894, Society of Colonial Wars; New England Genealogical and Historical Register, Vol. 37, p. 74.

25.   Frank Baker.
57.   Charles Clarence Poole.

LIEUTENANT THOMAS CUTLER.—[1648-1722]—Lieutenant of the Lexington Company.

REFERENCE: Hudson's History of Lexington, p. 49.

25.   Frank Baker.

RICHARD CUTT.—Came from England prior to 1646; died 1676; was made Captain in command of fort built at Great Island, 1660; represented Portsmouth several times in the General Court between 1655 and 1676.

REFERENCE: Adam's Portsmouth, p. 48; History of Cutt family.

46.   George Butters.

LIEUTENANT ELIHU DAGGETT.—Oct. 16, 1754, Lieutenant in Capt. John Stearnes' Company; April 6, 1757, private in Capt. John Stearnes' Company, alarm soldiers.

REFERENCE: French and Indian War Rolls; Vol. 93, p. 142; Vol. 95, p. 261.

66. Daniel Charles Daggett.

SAMUEL DAMON.—A soldier in the Narragansett or King Philip's War from Reading, Mass.

REFERENCE: Mass. Archives, Vol. 68, p. 79-100

39. George Samuel Marsh.

DEPUTY GOV. THOMAS DANFORTH.—(1622-1699.) Cambridge. Deputy Governor of Massachusetts in 1676-1692.

REFERENCE: 1896 Year Book, 308.

64. Harry Jenkins Bardwell.

MAJOR GENERAL DANIEL DENISON.—Massachusetts Colonial forces, who was appointed Captain (during the Pequot War), 1637, and Major General from 1652 to 1680. Deputy to the General Court, 1635-52. Colonial Secretary, 1653. Commissioner for the United Colonies, 1654-62.

REFERENCE: Society of Colonial Wars Year Book, 1895, p. 216; Savage's Gen. Dict.

54. William Ward Wight.

CAPTAIN GEORGE DENISON.—Captain of Roxbury, Mass., train band, 1646; campaigned against Narragansetts, 1654, also 1675; was at "Swamp Fight." In 1676 was appointed by Connecticut Council second in command of all Connecticut forces; was deputy to Legislature fifteen different times, 1671-1694.

REFERENCE: Society of Colonial Wars Year Book, 1894, p. 30-83; Connecticut Colonial Records, 1662-94.

10. Edward Milton Adams.

51. Franklin Adams Meacham.

GEORGE DENISON, JR.—Was appointed Commissary of Connecticut forces in New London County, 1703.

REFERENCE: Connecticut Colonial Records, Vol. 1689-1706, p. 438.

10. Edward Milton Adams.

51. Franklin Adams Meacham.

JOHN DENISON.—Of Stonington, Conn., was Ensign in Colonial forces, Aug. 7, 1673 and later; Was Deputy many years.

REFERENCE: Connecticut Colonial Records, 1665, p. 206.
10.   Edward Milton Adams.
51.   Franklin Adams Meacham.

DANIEL DENNY.—Captain of Militia at Leicester, Mass.; representative to the General Court, 1745-46-47.

REFERENCE: History of Leicester, Mass., 1860; Denny Genealogy, 1886.
5.   John Smith Sargent.

BALTHASAR DE WOLF.—Of Lyme, Conn. 1668, Member of the Lyme Train Band.

REFERENCE: Soc. Col. Wars Year Book, 1896, p. 310.
71.   Ebenezer Lane.

EBENEZER DIBBLE.—(1641-1675.) Killed in Great Swamp Fight, King Philip's War.

REFERENCE: Stiles' Ancient Windsor, Vol. 1, p. 225; Vol. 2, p. 174.
93.   Wyllys King Smith.

NATHANIEL DICKENSON.—(—— 1676.) Member of the Hampshire Troop under Capt. John Pynchon at its formation in 1663.

REFERENCES: Sheldon, pp. 1-19-159; Savage, Vol. 2, p. 48.
REFERENCE: Morton Memoranda (Leach) p. 134.
64.   Harry Jenkins Bardwell.
93.   Wyllys King Smith.

SERGT. OBADIAH DICKENSON.—(1641-1698.) One of the founders of Hatfield and one of the first members of the Hampshire Troop. His house was burned by Indians September 19, 1677. His wife wounded and himself and daughter carried to Canada, whence he returned next year.

REFERENCE: Morton's Memoranda (Leach) p. 136.
93.   Wyllys King Smith.

SERGT. JOHN DICKINSON.—(——1676.) Of Hadley; slain in the "Falls Fight" in King Philip's war. Leader of a band of twelve volunteers from Hatfield.

REFERENCES: Sheldon's Deerfield, Vol. 1, pp. 154 and 159; S. C. Wars, 1896, Year Book, page 310.
64.   Harry Jenkins Bardwell.

JOSEPH DICKINSON.—(—— 1675.) Of Northfield, Mass. A member of Capt. Beer's Company that went from Hadley, Mass., to Northfield for the purpose of rescuing the garrison stationed there. Most of the company, including Joseph Dickinson, were killed on the 4th of September, 1675, by the Indians.

REFERENCES: Mass. Archives, Vol. 67, p. 254; Bodge's Soldiers in King Philip's War; N. E. H. and G. R., Vol. 38, p. 329; History of Northfield, Mass., pp. 71-74; Judd's History of Hadley, p. 143.

96. Oliver Partridge Dickinson.

CAPT. ABRAHAM DICKERMAN.—(1634-1711.) Lieutenant New Haven Train Band.

REFERENCE: Colonial Records of Conn., 1698 to 1706, p. 24.

93. Wyllys King Smith.

CAPT. ISAAC DICKERMAN.—(1677-1758.) Captain of the New Haven Train Band, 1722.

REFERENCE: Colonial Records of Conn., 1717 to 1725, p. 341.

93. Wyllys King Smith.

JOHN DOANE.—[1591-1686]—Of Plymouth and Eastham; Governor's Assistant, 1632-3; Governor's Assistant, 1639, "to make laws for the Colony;" member of Plymouth Military Company, 1643; Deputy from Plymouth, 1639-42; from Eastham, 1649-50-53-59.

REFERENCE: Plymouth Colony Records, Vol. 1, p. 5-121; Pierce's Colonial Lists, p. 76.

18. Scott Jordan.

COMMISSARY WILLIAM DOUGLAS.—[1610-1682]—Gloucester and Boston, Mass., and New London, Conn. Commissioner of New London, 1667; Representative to the General Court, 1672, and thereafter; Commissary to the army during King Philip's War.

REFERENCE: Savage's Gen. Dict. of N. E.; Connecticut Colonial Records, Vol. 4, p. 289; Vol. 2, p. 442-455; Vol. 6, p. 489; Vol. 7, p. 468; Caulkin's History of New London.

68. Albert Judson Fisher.
96. Oliver Partridge Dickinson.

LIEUTENANT JOHN DRESSER.—[1639-1721]—Member of the Provincial forces of Massachusetts Bay. Deputy, 1691, and for several years thereafter from Rowley, Mass.

REFERENCE: Society of Colonial Wars Year Book, 1895, p. 218.
6. Lyman Dresser Hammond.

CAPTAIN RICHARD DRESSER.—[1714-1797]—Captain of the Charlton, Mass., Company in Col. John Chandler's Regiment, that marched to the relief of Ft. William Henry, Aug. 10, 1758, French and Indian War.

REFERENCE: Massachusetts Archives, Vol. 95, p. 519.
6. Lyman Dresser Hammond.

ABRAHAM DU BOIS.—Served in the second Canadian expedition against the French.

REFERENCE: New York Colonial Manuscripts, English, Vol. 60, p. 188.
13. Samuel Eberly Gross.

LOUIS DUBOIS.—French Huguenot settler and patentee of large land tract in eastern New York. Founder of the Huguenot settlement, New Paltz, in Ulster County. His wife, Catherine (Blanshan) DuBois, and her three children, with others, were carried into captivity by the Indians at the burning of Hurley (New Village), June 7, 1663. Louis DuBois led an expedition against the Indians, which defeated them in battle and effected the rescue of the captives. In 1670 he served again in the Colonial forces against the Indians, who were then on the war path. Was Magistrate in 1673, and after, at New Village and Marbleton; also was founder and First Elder of the French Reform Church of New Paltz.

REFERENCE: "American Ancestry," Vol. 1, p. 24-25; J. B. Beers' "History of Green County, New York;" Brodhead's "History of New York," Vol. 1, p. 657-678-711-714; Ibid., Vol. 2, p. 311-312; N. Y. Historic Documents, Vol. 13, p. 338-350; N. Y. Col. Archives, Vol. 13, p. 450; N. Y. Col. Archives, Vol. 13, p. 448; Schoonmaker's His. of Kingston, N. Y., p. 41-60-71-72-243-478.
13. Samuel Eberly Gross.

LIEUTENANT SOLOMON DUBOIS.—Lieutenant of the Ulster County Militia during early Colonial wars, given in list of the "Commanding Officers as well Milletery and Sivel," in 1728; in an Ulster County roster of "Old Ofesers and Old Men," as the name was spelled at that time: Lieut Sallomon DuBoys.

REFERENCE: Documentary History of the State of New York, Vol. 2, p. 588.
13. Samuel Eberly Gross.

FRANCIS DUDLEY.—A soldier in King Philip's War.

REFERENCE: Society of Colonial Wars Year Book, 1894, p. 53; Spooner Genealogy; Dudley Genealogy; Putnam's Monthly Historical Magazine.

49. Frank Eugene Spooner.

GOVERNOR THOMAS DUDLEY.—Came to America in 1630; was Governor or Deputy Governor of Massachusetts Bay Colony from 1634 to 1640, being third Governor of the Colony. Assistant, 1635-36-41-44. Continuously in office 22 years. Commissioner for the United Colonies, 1643-47-49. Twice President of the United Colonies, Major General or commander of all the military forces in the Colony in 1644 and was again Governor from 1645 to 1650.

REFERENCE: Society of Colonial Wars Year Book, 1895, p. 60 and 219; Massachusetts Colonial Records, 1630-1653; Appleton's Cyclopedia of American Biography, p. 243; Savage's Genealogical Dictionary; Ruggles Genealogy, p. 141-2-3; Humphrey Genealogy; Dudley Genealogy; Woodbridge Genealogy; New England Historical and Genealogical Register; Suffield, Conn., Simsbury, Conn., Norfolk, Conn., town and church records; Southfield, Mass., church records.

4. William Ruggles Tucker.
5. John Smith Sargent.
10. Edward Milton Adams.
19. Jonathan Edwards Woodbridge.
24. Lemuel Ruggles Hall.
54. William Ward Wight.
57. Charles Clarence Poole.
96. Oliver Partridge Dickinson.
101. John Newbury Bagley.

JOHN DUMBLETON, JR.—[1658-1675]—Killed by Indians during King Philip's War at Westfield, Mass., Oct. 27, 1675.

REFERENCE: Savage's Gen. Dict.; History of Hadley, p. 156, by Judd; Holland's "History of Western Mass.," p. 106-107; Sprague's Historic Address, p. 24; Markham's "History of King Philip's War," p. 123-155; Hubbard's "Indian Wars in New England," p. 127.

68. Albert Judson Fisher.

WILLIAM EAGER.—(Ager, Agur) was private in Capt. Thomas Prentiss' Company of "Middlesex" troopers in Mt. Hope campaign; his name appears on roll of Aug. 27, 1675; he was also in same company under Lieut. Edward Oakes, 1675-6.

REFERENCE: N. E. Hist. and Gen. Reg., Vol. 47, p. 280-4.

52. Hobart Chatfield Chatfield-Taylor.

THOMAS EAMES.—(1618-1680.) Framingham, Mass. A soldier in the war 1637; his house was burned by the Indians February, 1676-7. His wife and some of his children killed.

REFERENCE: Barry's History of Framingham, Mass., p. 227.
99. Eames Mac Veagh.

SAMUEL EDDY.—Of Plymouth, Mass.; member of the Plymouth Military Company in August, 1643.

REFERENCE: Pierce's Colonial Lists, p. 76.
67. John Demmon Vandercook.

ROBERT ELLIOTT.—Representative to General Court; President of Council of Province of N. H.

REFERENCE: Provincial Records, N. H.; Savage's Dictionary.
46. George Butters.

EDWARD ELMER, SR.—A soldier in King Philip's War, and killed in June, 1676.

REFERENCE: S. C. W. 1895 Year Book.
39. George Samuel Marsh.

SERGEANT JOHN EMERY, JR.—[1629-1693]—Of Newbury, Mass.; soldier under Major Samuel Appleton, Dec. 19, 1675, at the "Great Swamp Fight." Served in Capt. Samuel Brocklebank's Company.

REFERENCE: Soldiers of King Philip's War, 1675-7, p. 109-159-310; Coffin's History of Newbury, p. 145; N. E. Hist. and Gen. Register, Vol. 27, p. 423.
2. Captain Philip Reade.

CAPTAIN JOHN EVERETT.—[1636-1714]—Dedham, Mass. In 1695 commanded a company of fifty or sixty Massachusetts soldiers, raised and sent by the Massachusetts Colony to assist the New Hampshire Colony against the Indians. Stationed at Exeter and Portsmouth, N. H., and after eleven months ordered into Maine.

REFERENCE: Savage's Genealogical Dictionary; N. H. Provincial Papers, Vol. 11, p. 153-157-158-169; "Acts and Resolves of the Province of Mass. Bay," Vol. 7; Resolves, 1692-1702, Appendix 2, p. 521.
68. Albert Judson Fisher.
82. Marvin Andrus Farr.

GABRIEL FALLOWELL.—A member of the Plymouth Military Company in August, 1643.

REFERENCE: Pierce's Colonial Lists, p. 76.
61. Victor Clifton Alderson.

LIEUTENANT DAVID FARNSWORTH.—[1711 ——]—Of Charlestown and Hollis, N. H. On April 20, 1757, he was taken prisoner by party of seventy French and Indians, and carried to Canada. Some years later he was redeemed and returned home.

REFERENCE: Farnsworth Genealogy, p. 87; Saunderson's History of Charlestown, p. 14-335.
    4. William Ruggles Tucker.

MATTHIAS FARNSWORTH.—Of Groton. Served in 1675 with Maj. Willard. His home was burned by the Indians in 1676, and the family took refuge in Concord.

REFERENCE: History of Groton; Bodge's Soldiers in King Philip's War, pp. 121 and 436.
    4. William Ruggles Tucker.
   67. John Demmon Vandercook.
   82. Marvin Andrus Farr.

SAMUEL FARNSWORTH.—[1669 ——]—A member of the Garrison of Groton, Mass., March 17, 1691-2.

REFERENCE: N. E. Hist. and Gen. Register for 1889, p. 374.
    4. William Ruggles Tucker.

STEPHEN FARNSWORTH.—Was captured by the Indians, April 19, 1746, and taken to Montreal, where he was confined. He was also one of Capt. Stevens' company, raised for the defense of "No. 4;" company formed June 21, 1750.

REFERENCE: History of Charlestown, N. H., p. 342.
   67. John Demmon Vandercook.

STEPHEN FARR.—Served in King Philip's War; from Concord, 1675-1676, in Capt. Davenport's Company.

REFERENCE: N. E. H. & G. R., Vol. 39, p. 256; Bodge's Soldiers in King Philip's War, p. 170.
   82. Marvin Andrus Farr.

JACOB FARRAR.—One of the seven victims killed and mutilated by the Indians in Monaco's raid upon Lancaster, Aug. 27, 1675, during King Philip's War.

REFERENCE: Nourse's "Military Annals of Lancaster," p. 10; Savage's Genealogical Dictionary; Year Book Society of Colonial Wars, 1895; Marvin's History of Lancaster, p. 59-102.
   68. Albert Judson Fisher.

JOHN FIELD.—Was a soldier under Capt. Turner in the "Falls Fight" in King Philip's War.

REFERENCE: Sheldon, Vol. 2, p. 156.
   64. Harry Jenkins Bardwell.

CAPT. JOSEPH FIELD.—(1658-1736.) Hatfield and Deerfield. Was a captain in the Indian wars.

REFERENCE: Sheldon, Vol. 2, p. 156.
64. Harry Jenkins Bardwell.

ZACHARIAH FIELD.—(—— 1666.) One of the 37 soldiers from Hartford that served in the Pequot War.

REFERENCE: 1896 Year Book p. 316.
64. Harry Jenkins Bardwell.

ANTHONY FISHER, JR.—[—— 1670]—Dedham, Mass., in 1637; member of Ancient and Honorable Artillery Company in 1644.

REFERENCE: Savage's Genealogical Dictionary; Whitman's History of A. and H. Artillery Company, p. 143; Mass. Bay Colonial Records. Vol. 4, part 1, p. 117.
68. Albert Judson Fisher.

NATHANIEL FISKE.—September 3, 1675, credited with £1 13s 0d for services performed in Capt. Daniel Henchman's Company in King Philip's War.

REFERENCE: Bodge's Soldiers in King Philip's War, p. 52.
4. William Ruggles Tucker.
67. John Demmon Vandercook.

REV. JAMES FITCH.—(1622-1702.) Chaplain of the Connecticut forces in the "Great Swamp Fight" in King Philip's War. Appointed chaplain of forces under Major Treat in January, 1675. Requested to accompany Major John Talcott in May, 1676. Appointed by the General Court of Connecticut to secure the fidelity of the Indian Allies.

REFERENCE: Ancient Windsor II., p. 261, Conn. Col. Records, Vol. 1665-1677, pp. 400, 402, 421, 422, 279, 447, 448, 336, 346, 349, 371 and 381.
64. Harry Jenkins Bardwell.

MAJ. JAMES FITCH.—(1649-1727.) Assistant Governor, Colony of Connecticut twenty-six years, 1681-1706. Commissioner to receive land from Uncas. Sent to New York to confer with Capt. Jacob Leisler, Captain of Norwich Train Band, 1680. Served in the Indian wars and against the French, 1702. Commissioned Sergeant Major of New London, 1696. Placed in command of the fort at New London and all the troops in that county, with general orders to protect the life and property of his Majesty's subjects, 1697.

REFERENCES: Ancient Windsor II., p. 262; Savage II., p. 163; 1896 Year Book, p. 317; Conn. Col. Records, Vol. 1678-1689, pp. 44, 60, 75, 96, 114, 139, 168, 194, 229, 250, 255, Vol. 1689-1706, pp. 23, 189, 219, 531.
64. Harry Jenkins Bardwell.

CAPT. JOHN FITCH.—(1667-1743.) Commissioned Lieutenant of Windham Train Band, 1695; made Captain of the same company, 1703. Deputy, 20 sessions; town clerk, 38 years.

REFERENCES: Ancient Windsor II., p. 262; Conn. Col. Records, Vol. 1689-1706, pp. 149, 445.

64. Harry Jenkins Bardwell.

CAPT. JOHN FITCH, JR.—(1705-1750.) Captain of the militia. Commissioned Lieutenant of Windham Train Band, 1730. Deputy, seven sessions for Windham and Canterbury.

REFERENCES: Ancient Windsor II., p. 263; Conn. Col. Records, Vol. 1726-1735, pp. 272, 88, 120, 123, 193, 250, 266, 403.

64. Harry Jenkins Bardwell.

WILLIAM FITZHUGH.—Of "Bedford," Stafford County, Va. Was Lieutenant-Colonel of Westmoreland County, 1683; member of House of Burgesses, 1678-1687; Colonel of Stafford County forces 1690.

REFERENCES: Society of Colonial Wars Year Book, 1896, p. 317; Cabells and Their Kin, A. Brown, p. 215.

74. Hiram Holbrook Rose.

91. Landon Cabell Rose.

LIEUTENANT JOHN FLINT.—Lieutenant in Capt. Thomas Hinchman's troop, composed of troopers in Sudbury, Marlborough, Concord, Mass. Was a deputy from Concord, Mass., to serve at the General Court.

REFERENCE: Official Records of the General Court of Massachusetts, Vol. 5, p. 132-210-260-350-1; Genealogical Register of the Descendants of Thomas Flint of Salem; History of Antrim, p. 495.

56. Wyman Kneeland Flint.

THOMAS FLINT.—(1603-1653.) One of the first settlers of Concord, Mass., and Magistrate for many years. His will was the first probated in Middlesex County.

REFERENCES: Savage's Gen. Dict., p. 75; N. E. Hist. and Gen. Reg., Vol. 1, p. 286.

56. Wyman Kneeland Flint.

SERGEANT THOMAS FLINT.—Of Salem Village, Danvers, Mass., in 1638, and of Redding, after 1644. Was in Capt. Joseph Gardiner's troop, Dec. 10-16, 1675; also in Capt. Curwin's troop and in the troop commanded by Capt. Thomas Prentice. Was in the Reserve Salem Old Troop.

REFERENCE: Mass. Archives, Vol. 68, p. 73-93-104-119, also Vol. 69, p. 217; Bodge, p. 41-117-118; Gen. History of Reading, Mass., by Lilley Eaton, 1874; Gen. Reg. Descendants of Thos. Flint of Salem, p. 10-11, by John Flint, and J. H. Stone.

2. Capt. Philip Reade.

GERRIT FOKAR.—Served in Capt. Pawling's foot company of Hurley soldiers, doing duty at Marbleton, N. Y., during Esopus Indian Wars.

REFERENCE: New York Colonial Manuscripts, Vol. 22, p. 99 and following; New York Historical Documents, Vol. 13, p. 246 and following.

13.   Samuel Eberly Gross.

NATHANIEL FOOTE.—(1648-1703.)   Hadley.   Quartermaster of Capt. William Turner's Company in the "Falls Fight," May 19, 1676, in King Philip's War.

REFERENCE: Bodge's Soldiers in King Philip's War, pp. 250-253.

48.   Henry Austin Osborn.
64.   Harry Jenkins Bardwell.

EDMUND FREEMAN.—[1589-1682]—Of Sandwich, Mass.; member of Colonial "War" Council, Sept. 27, 1642; Assistant Plymouth Colony, 1640-45; member of council of war to provide troops for the safety of the Colony against the Indians, 1642, Plymouth Colony.

REFERENCE: Pierce's Colonial Lists, p. 4-85, also Plymouth Colonial Records, Vol. 1, p. 140.

50.   Albert Eugene Snow.
58.   Frederick Laforrest Merrick.
61.   Victor Clifton Alderson.
90.   Edwin Fraser Gillette.

JOHN FREEMAN.—Was a member of Military Company, Sandwich, Mass., 1643; commissioned Ensign at Eastham, March, 1655; Lieutenant of Cavalry Company; commissioned Oct. 2, 1659; Assistant of Plymouth Colony, 1667, 1678 and 1682-86; was Lieutenant and second in command under Major Josiah Winslow, who, with 102 men, marched against Awashouk, the Squaw, Sachem, of Saconett, near Assonet, July 8, 1671; was member of Eastham town "War" Council, Feb. 29, 1675; was appointed Major of 3d Plymouth Colony Regiment, composed of companies from Barnstable, Eastham, Sandwich and Yarmouth.

REFERENCE: Pierce's Colonial Lists, p. 68-73-94-97-98; Plymouth Colonial Records, Vol. 3, p. 74-174; Vol. 4, p. 147; N. E. H. and G. Register, Vol. 20, p. 59-60.

50.   Albert Eugene Snow.
58.   Frederick Laforrest Merrick.
61.   Victor Clifton Alderson.
90.   Edwin Fraser Gillette.

JACOB FRENCH.—[1640-1713]—Of Billerica; Sergeant of the Militia. His house used as a garrison house in 1676.

REFERENCE: N. E. Hist. and Gen. Register, Vol. 44, p. 368.

73. Anthony French Merrill.

CORPORAL JOHN FRENCH.—Was wounded by the Indians in the assault at Quaboag in 1675.

REFERENCE: Society of Colonial Wars Year Book, 1895, p. 221.

63. Rev. Abbott Eliot Kittredge.

LIEUT. WILLIAM FRENCH.—(1603-1681.) Of Cambridge and Billerica, Mass. Was commissioned Lieutenant at Cambridge, May 26, 1647. A member of the Ancient and Honorable Artillery Company of Boston in 1638. Junior Sergeant in 1643. First Sergeant in 1646 and Ensign in 1650. Representative from Billerica in 1660 and 1663. Captain of an Artillery Company in Billerica at the time of his death in 1681.

REFERENCES: Mass. Archives, Vol. 3, p. 109; Roberts' Hist. of Ancient and Honorable Artillery Co., p. 60.

1. Seymour Morris.
52. Hobart Chatfield Chatfield-Taylor.
63. Rev. Abbott Eliot Kittredge.
75. Anthony French Merrill.

WILLIAM FRENCH—[1701-1775]—He was Lieutenant and served in war against the Indians, being on the muster roll of 1722.

REFERENCE: N. E. Hist. and Gen. Register, Vol. 44, p. 371.

73. Anthony French Merrill.

CAPT. MATTHEW FULLER.—Was the eighth Captain after Miles Standish in Plymouth Colony Troop.

REFERENCES: Bodge's Soldiers in King Philip's War; Savage's Gen. Dict., Vol. 3.

56. Wyman Kneeland Flint.

THOMAS FULLER.—Was Sergeant in 1656. Lieutenant in 1685 in Woburn and Wenham, Mass.

REFERENCE: Sewall's History of Woburn, p. 614; Massachusetts Colonial Records, Vol. 5, p. 56.

17. Frederick Clifton Pierce.

LION GARDINER.—(1599-1663.) Lieutenant in English Army. Engineer and Master of Works of Fortification in Leagues of the Prince of Orange in the Low Countries. Engineer at Boston. Constructor and commander of Saybrook Fort, Pequot War. First Englishman seated in New York. Lord of the Isle of Wight, and now called Gardiner's Island.

REFERENCES: Lion Gardiner and His Descendants; Society of Colonial Wars, 1896, Yearbook; Magazine of American History, Vol. 13, pp. 1 to 30.
7. Edward McKinstry Teall.
56. Wyman Kneeland Flint.

SIMON GATES.—Received a grant of land in Narragansett township, November 2, for his services in King Philip's Wars.

REFERENCES: Bodge's History of King Philip's War, p. 417, 1896; History of Lancaster Wars; History of Marlboro Wars.
5. John Smith Sargent.

JOHN GERRISH.—[1646-1714]—Chosen Representative to General Court, 1684; member of convention, 1689; also Captain and Sheriff

REFERENCE: Savage's Dictionary, N. E. H. and G., Vol. 6, p. 258.
46. George Butters.

COLONEL TIMOTHY GERRISH.—[1684-1756]—Dover, N. H. Captain of the Provincial Militia at Dover, 1719. Deputy, 1709-15-22. Colonel of the Provincial Militia of York County, Me., 1725. Royal Councillor of Province of Massachusetts, 1730-1735.

REFERENCE: Society of Colonial Wars Year Book, 1895, p. 225.
46. George Butters.

COLONEL JAMES GIBSON.—A retired British army officer, equipped at his own expense a company of 300 men and led them at the siege of Louisburg, Cape Breton in 1745.

REFERENCE: Windsor Memorial History of Breton, Vol. 2, p. 113-117; Parkman, Half Century of Conflict, Vol. 2, p. 85-100; Drake, "The Taking of Louisburg," p. 70; Year Book, Society of Colonial Wars, 1894, p. 209.
32. Rev. James Gibson Johnson.

JOHN GILBERT.—[—— 1654]—Of Dorchester and Taunton, Mass. In 1643 a member of the Military Company of Yarmouth, Mass., commanded by Lieut. Wm. Palmer.

REFERENCE: Pierce's Colonial List, p. 75.
4. William Ruggles Tucker.

JONATHAN GILBERT.—Rendered important services in the Indian wars. He was sent to one of the rebellious chiefs, Sequasson, by the Commissioners to summon him to their presence. He and John Griffin were sent as messengers to Chief Chickwallop and Manasanes by the Commissioners, but the Sagamores and Indians at Waranoke carried it insolently, etc. Sent by the Commissioners as a messenger to the chief of the Narragansetts during hostilities in 1652. Was sent by the Commissioners to chiefs of the Podunk Indians during hostilities in 1657.

REFERENCE: N. E. Reg., Vol. 4, p. 229-230-231-232.

36. Henry Lathrop Turner.
77. James Harris Gilbert.

LIEUT. NATHANIEL GILBERT.—(1689-1756.) Middletown, Conn. Served under Capt. Moses Demming in the expedition against Canada in 1709. In May, 1736, was confirmed Lieutenant of the Military Company at "Newfield in the town of Middletown."

REFERENCE: Connecticut Colonial Records, Vol. 8, p. 33.

77. James Harris Gilbert.

CAPT. NATHANIEL GILBERT.—(1723-1787.) Middletown, Conn., and Herkimer County, New York. In May, 1760, appointed Lieutenant of the Eleventh (Middletown) Company of the Sixth Connecticut Colonial Regiment; and in May, 1765, he was made Captain of the same company.

REFERENCES: Connecticut Colonial Records, Vol. 8, p. 277; Vol. 12, p. 350.

77. James Harris Gilbert.

SAMUEL GILLETT.—(1643-1676.) Of Hatfield. Was killed by the Indians at the great "Falls Fight" in King Philip's War, May 19, 1676.

REFERENCES: Sheldon I., p. 159; Savage II., p. 256.

64. Harry Jenkins Bardwell.

SAMUEL GILLETT, JR.—Of Hatfield, Mass. Died 1769. A soldier at the battle of Deerfield Meadow, February, 1703.

REFERENCE: Sheldon's Deerfield I., p. 298.

64. Harry Jenkins Bardwell.

CAPTAIN EDWARD GODDARD.—[1675-1754]—Captain of troop; Deputy to General Court from Framingham, Mass., 1724-1731; three years in his Majesty's Council, 1733-36.

REFERENCE: Town records of Framingham, Mass.
31.   Charles Newton Fessenden.

EDMOND GOODENOW.—(1611-1676.)   Captain of company from Sudbury, Mass. King Philip's War.

REFERENCE: Soldiers in King Philip' ''ar, by Bodge, pp. 224, 227, 230 and 474.
105.   Henry Clay Fuller.

JOHN GOODENOW.—(1634-1721.)   In company from Sudbury, Mass., in King Philip's War.

REFERENCE: Soldiers of King Philip's War, by Bodge, p. 225.
105.   Henry Clay Fuller.

RICHARD GOODMAN.—Was elected inspector of arms at Hadley, Mass., on Dec. 16, 1664; was appointed by the County Court Sergeant of the Hadley Military Company in 1663; was killed by the Indians at Hockanum (near Northampton), Mass., on April 1, 1676, King Philip's War.

REFERENCE: Judd's History of Hadley, Mass., p. 165-226.
43.   Harry Linn Wright.
52.   Hobart Chatfield Chatfield-Taylor.
89.   Albert Mattoon Graves.

ENSIGN WILLIAM GOODRICH.—(—— 1676.)   Ensign of the Wethersfield Train Band, commanded by Capt. Samuel Wells, Deputy, 1660-1666.

REFERENCE: S. C. W. 1896 Year Book, p. 324.
93.   Wyllys King Smith.
99.   Eames Mac Veagh.

CAPTAIN PHILIP GOODRIDGE.—Captain of Company in French and Indian War, 1755.

REFERENCE: Massachusetts Archives.
31.   Charles Newton Fessenden.

JABEZ GORHAM.—(1656——.)   Son of Capt. John Gorham. Wounded in King Philip's War.

REFERENCE: Savage, Vol. 2, p. 281.
93.   Wyllys King Smith.

CAPTAIN JOHN GORHAM.—Commanded second Plymouth Colony Company in Great Swamp Fight, 1675.

REFERENCE: Plymouth Colony Records, 1650-1676; S. C. W. 1894 Year Book.

10. Edward Milton Adams.
51. Franklin Adams Meacham.
93. Wyllys King Smith.

SAMUEL GORTON.—Of Warwick, R. I. In 1649 Assistant; 1651-56-63, Commissioner; 1664-66-70, Deputy.

REFERENCE: Austin's Genealogical Dictionary of Rhode Island, p. 394.

39. George Samuel Marsh.
75. Warren Lippitt Beckwith.

BENJAMIN GRAVES.—[1645 ——]—Of Concord, Mass.; soldier in Capt. Wheeler's Company in the Great Swamp Fight, 1675.

REFERENCE: N. E. Hist. and Gen. Register, Vol. 38, p. 40.

1. Seymour Morris.

ISAAC GRAVES.—(1620-1677.) Of Hatfield, Mass. Killed by the Indians at the time they attacked the settlement at Hatfield.

REFERENCES: Soldiers in King Philip's War, by Bodge, pp. 152, 242 and 244; Graves' Genealogy, Vol. 1, pp. 1 to 10.

89. Albert Mattoon Graves.

JOHN GRAVES.— (——1677.) Of Wethersfield, Conn., and Hatfield, Mass. Was killed by the Indians in their attack upon Hatfield, September 19, 1677.

REFERENCES: Graves' Genealogy, p. 11; Boltwood's History of Hadley Families, p. 61.

99. Eames Mac Veagh.

JOHN GREEN.—Was a member of Lieut. Edward Oakes' troop in the winter of 1675-76. He was also Corporal under Lieut. William Hasey, August to October, 1675, King Philip's War.

REFERENCE: New England Historical and Genealogical Register, Vol. 37, p. 284; Vol. 42, p. 94.

17. Frederick Clifton Pierce.

DEPUTY-GOVERNOR   JOHN   GREENE. — (1620-1708.)
Commissioner to the General Court, 1652-63.   Attorney-General, 1657-60.   Assistant, seven terms, 1660-90.   Colonial
Agent to England, 1670.   Member of Governor Andros' Council, 1686.   Deputy nine terms, 1664-80.   "Major for the Main"
1696.   Deputy-Governor, 1690-1700.   Captain, 1676.   Major,
1683, Colony of Rhode Island.

REFERENCE: S. C. W. Year Book, 1896, p. 327.
75.   Warren Lippitt Beckwith.

THOMAS GREENE, SR.—(1628-1717.)   Assistant, Colony
of Rhode Island.

REFERENCE: S. C. W. Year Book, 1896, p. 327.
75.   Warren Lippitt Beckwith.

CAPT. EDMOND GREENLEAF.—(1600-1671.)   Of Newbury, Mass.   Member of Massachusetts Colonial forces.   Lieutenant in 1642.   Captain 1645 of the Newbury Company.

REFERENCES: S. C. W., 1896 Year Book, p. 327.
88.   Edward Payson Bailey.

THOMAS GRIDLEY.—Was soldier from Connecticut in
the Pequot War, 1637, in Capt. John Mason's Company.

REFERENCES: S. C. W. Year Book, 1895, p. 230; Soldiers in
King Philip's War, by Bodge, p. 466.
33.   Deming Haven Preston.
96.   Oliver Partridge Dickinson.
100.   Nelson Cowles Gridley.

JOHN GRIFFIN.—Of Windsor.   Deputy, 1670.   Appointed
by the Legislature temporary commander of the Simsbury
Train Band, 1673, confirmed Sergeant and Chief in command,
1675.

REFERENCE: Mass. and Conn. Colonial Records; Stiles' History of Windsor; Humphrey Genealogy.
10.   Edward Milton Adams.
33.   Deming Haven Preston.

EDWARD GRISWOLD.—Built "Old Fort" Springfield; Deputy to General Court from Windsor and Killingworth for many
years.

REFERENCE: Ancient Windsor ——, Vol. 7, p. 350-351.
42.   Charles Thomson Atkinson.

LIEUTENANT MATTHEW GRISWOLD.—[1620-1698]—Of Windsor and Lyme, Conn. Lieutenant of the Lyme Train Band. Deputy, 1654-1667, 1668, 1678, 1685.

REFERENCE: Connecticut Colonial Records, 1678-1689, p. 3-27-181; Magazine of American History, Vol. 11, p. 131.

71. Ebenezer Lane.
78. Joseph Edward Otis, Jr.
98. Philo Adams Otis.

GOVERNOR MATTHEW GRISWOLD.—[1714-1789]—In 1739 Captain of the South Train Band of Lyme, Conn.; 1766, Major of Third Regiment of Horse and Foot; 1751, Representative; 1759-1765, member of Governor's Council; 1766-69, Chief Justice; 1771-84, Deputy Governor and Lieutenant Governor of Connecticut; 1784-86, Governor.

REFERENCE: Magazine of American History, Vol. 11, p. 218-237.

71. Ebenezer Lane.

JOHN GUILD.—A soldier in Capt. Appleton's Company, King Philip's War.

REFERENCE: S. C. W. Year Book, page 329; Bodge, p. 157.

82. Marvin Andrus Farr.

JAMES HADLOCK.—Served in Capt. Holbrook's Company in King Philip's War, August 24, 1676.

REFERENCE: N. E. Hist. and Gen. Register, Vol. 42, p. 99.

6. Lyman Dresser Hammond.
24. Lemuel Ruggles Hall.

CAPTAIN WALTER HAINES.—[1583-1655]—Of Watertown, Mass., 1638; Sudbury, 1639; built the Haines Garrison on the west side, which sustained the burden of the fight in the memorable Indian attack upon Sudbury during King Philip's War, April 21, 1675; member of the Ancient and Honorable Artillery Company in 1639; Representative for Sudbury from 1641 to 1651.

REFERENCE: Hudson's "Annals of Sudbury, Wayland and Maynard," p. 4-8-10-13-14-15; Whitman's "History Ancient" Honorable Artillery Co., Ed. 1842, p. 97; N. E. Hist. and Gen. Register, Vol. 47, p. 72; Vol. 39, p. 263-264; Vol. 2, p. 108, Savage's Genealogical Dictionary; "Porter Family History," Vol. 1, p. 26.

68. Albert Judson Fisher.

CAPTAIN EZEKIEL HALE.—[1725-1789]—Of Newbury and Dracut, Mass. Served in the French War, 1758-61. In 1755 or 1756 went to Albany in Colonel Ephraim Williams' Regiment, in command of Sir William Johnson (Seven Years' War). He was a Lieutenant in the 6th Foot Company of Newbury in 1761.

REFERENCE: Genealogy of the Hale family, p. 180; New England Historical and Genealogical Register, Vol. 21, p. 83-98.

2. Captain Philip Reade.

SERGEANT THOMAS HALE.—[1633-1688]—Of Newbury, Mass., having been authorized "to carry on the military exercise there," was appointed, etc., 1652-57.

REFERENCE: Records of the Colony of Mass. Bay, Vol. 3, p. 290; Vol. 4, p. 117; N. E. Historical and Genealogical Register, Vol. 31; Hale Genealogy.

2. Captain Philip Reade.

CAPTAIN THOMAS HALE.—[1658-9-1730]—Of Newbury and Rowley, Mass., was Captain in the Militia.

REFERENCE: Genealogy of the descendants of Thomas Hale of Newbury, Massachusetts Archives, 114-178-450-501.

2. Captain Philip Reade.

EDWARD HALL.—(——1670.) Served in the Narragansett Expedition, 1645, from Duxborough, Mass.

REFERENCE: Soldiers in King Philip's War, p. 458.

79. John Whipple Hill.

JOHN HALL.—A member of the Barnstable Military Company in Plymouth Colony in August, 1643.

REFERENCE: Pierce's Colonial Lists, p. 73.

24. Lemuel Ruggles Hall.

ENSIGN JOHN HALL.—(1735-1812.) Wrentham. Member of Capt. Samuel Day's Company, Col. Miller's Regiment, April 22, 1757. Ensign in Capt. Samuel Cowell's Company, Third Suffolk Regiment (Col. Nathaniel Hatch), June, 1771.

REFERENCES: Mass. Archives, Vol. 95, p. 303; Vol. 99, p. 389.

79. John Whipple Hill.

SAMUEL HALL.—Served under Capt. Seely, in the Narragansett Fort Fight.

REFERENCE: Conn. Col. Records, Vol. 1678-1689, p. 5.

102. Marvin Allen Ives.

ANDREW HALLETT, SR.—Was in Lieut. William Palmer's Company at Yarmouth, Mass., Aug., 1643.

REFERENCE: Pierce's Colonial Lists, p. 74.

4. William Ruggles Tucker.
37. Frank Bassett Tobey.

SERGEANT EBENEZER HAMMOND.—[1714]—Of Charlton, Mass. Sergeant of a detachment of Capt. Jonathan Tooker's Company in Col. John Chandler's Regiment in the French and Indian War, marching to the relief of Ft. William Henry, under command of Joshua Meriam as their captain. Lieutenant of the First Regiment of Militia in County of Worcester, Mass., March 1, 1763, in Capt. Paul Wheelock's Company of Charlton.

REFERENCE: Massachusetts Archives, Vol. 95, p. 517; Vol. 99, p. 519.

6. Lyman Dresser Hammond.

SAMUEL HARLOW.—[1652 ——]—Sergeant in Commander James Warren's Plymouth South Company on Roll, 1699.

REFERENCE: History of Plymouth Co.; Davis Landmarks of Plymouth, p. 128

46. George Butters.

ENSIGN THOMAS HARRIS.—An Ensign in the Connecticut Colonial forces.

REFERENCE: Conn. Col. Records, Vol. 1665-1677, p. 304.

102. Marvin Allen Ives.

CAPTAIN THOMAS HART.—Of Farmington, Conn. Ensign, 1678; Lieutenant, 1693; Captain, 1695; Deputy, 1690-1711; Speaker, 1700-06.

REFERENCE: Society of Colonial Wars Year Book, 1895, p. 232.

33. Deming Haven Preston.

JOHN HARTSHORN.—Of Reading, Mass., and Rowley. Was credited £2 15s 0d for service in King Philip's War in Capt. Joseph Sill's Company.

REFERENCE: Bodge's Soldiers in King Philip's War, p. 274.
88. Edward Payson Bailey.

JOHN HASTINGS.—[1653 ——]—Of Watertown, Mass. A member of Capt. Davenport's Company in King Philip's War.

REFERENCE. N. E. Hist. and Gen. Register, Vol. 39, p. 259.
4. William Ruggles Tucker.
67. John Demmon Vandercook.

DR. THOMAS HASTINGS.—(1652-1712.)—Hatfield. A soldier under Capt. Richard Beers, February 29, 1675; also under Maj. Samuel Appleton, December 10, 1675.

REFERENCES: Bodge's Soldiers of King Philip's War; N. E. Hist. and Genealogical Register, Vol. 38, pp. 332-440.
64. Harry Jenkins Bardwell.

ABRAHAM HATHAWAY.—(1652-1725.)   Of Taunton, Mass. Credited on August 27, 1675, with £2 7s 0d for services performed under Capt. Daniel Henchman in King Philip's War.

REFERENCE: Bodge's Soldiers in King Philip's War, p. 52.
4. William Ruggles Tucker.

WILLIAM HATHORNE.—Of Salem, Mass. First Speaker of the House of Deputies, 1644; Assistant, 1662-79; Commissioner for the United Colonies in 1643; Captain of the Salem Company of Militia and Major of the Massachusetts Bay Colony, 1656.

REFERENCE: S. C. W. Year Book, p. 233.
30. Charles Durkee Dana.
83. Alfred Henry Castle.
90. Edwin Fraser Gillette.

SERGT. JOHN HAWKS.—Sent in pursuit of a party of Canadian Indians which had murdered settlers at Hatfield, under command of Capt. Thomas Watts, in 1697; active through King Philip's War; wounded in the "Falls Fight" and went to the aid of Hatfield, 1676.

REFERENCE: Sheldon's Deerfield, Vol. 1, pp. 159, 182, 321.
64. Harry Jenkins Bardwell.

ANTHONY HAWKINS.—One of the patentees of Connecticut under charter from Charles II., April 29, 1662; Assistant, 1668-70; Deputy.

REFERENCE: Savage's Genealogical Dictionary, p. 382; Colonial Wars Year Book, 1895.
42. Charles Thomson Atkinson.

CAPT. JOSEPH HAWLEY.—(1675-1752.) A member of the Connecticut Colonial Militia.

REFERENCE: S. C. W. Year Book, 1896.
96. Oliver Partridge Dickinson.

STEPHEN HAWLEY.—(1695-1790.) Of Stratford, New Milford and Newtown, Conn. A member of Capt. John Lover's Company of Newtown, Conn., in May, 1748.

REFERENCES: Conn. Col. Records, Vol. 9, p. 372; Hawley Genealogy, pp. 2, 256, 454 and 455; Savage's Gen. Dict., Vol. 2; History of Stratford, Conn.
80. Rev. Frank Wakely Gunsaulus.

JOHN HAYNES.—[1621-1692]—(Deacon). Was owner and Commander of a garrison house (block house) at Sudbury, Mass. Bay Colony. He served in Sir Wm. Phipps' Canadian expedition in 1690. Representative of Sudbury to General Const., 1668.

REFERENCE: Massachusetts Archives, Vol. 30, p. 205; New England Historical and Genealogical Register, Vol. 40, p. 398-399-400-403; Bodge's papers on King Philip's War; Hudson's Annals of Sudbury, p. 14-15-33, etc.; N. E. Hist. and Gen. Register, Vol. 47, p. 72; Savage's Gen. Dict. of N. E.
62. William Dorrance Messinger.
68. Albert Judson Fisher.

ELISHA HEDGE.—Appointed Sergeant on July 8, 1671, in Plymouth Colony.

REFERENCE: Pierce's Colonial Lists, p. 94.
37. Frank Bassett Tobey.

WILLIAM HEDGE.—Commissioner Ensign June 9, 1653, and Captain August 2, 1659, of the Yarmouth (Mass.) Company of the Plymouth Militia.

REFERENCE: Pierce's Colonial Lists, p. 69.
37. Frank Bassett Tobey.

JOHN HENRY.—Of Hanover County, Virginia. Was Presiding Magistrate of Hanover County, and Colonel of Militia. Was the father of Patrick Henry.

REFERENCES: Life of Patrick Henry, W. W. Henry, Vol. 1, p. 4; Life of Patrick Henry, William Wirt, p. 2.
74. Hiram Holbrook Rose.
91. Landon Cabell Rose.

CAPTAIN SAMUEL HICKOX.—[1695-1765]—Of Waterbury. Captain of the Militia.

REFERENCE: History of Waterbury, Conn.
  1. Seymour Morris.

SERGEANT SAMUEL HICKOX.—One of the original proprietors and grantee in the first Indian deed of Waterbury, Conn. Sergeant in the local militia.

REFERENCE: History of Waterbury, Conn.
  1. Seymour Morris.

CAPTAIN WILLIAM HICKOX.—[1673]—Of Waterbury, Conn.; an original proprietor; Captain of the Militia in 1727; Deputy to the General Court in 1728.

REFERENCE: History of Waterbury, Conn.
  1. Seymour Morris.

ZACHARIAH HICKS.—Was private in Capt. Joseph Sill's Company of Massachusetts Bay troops, Aug. 24, 1676.

REFERENCE: New England Historical and Genealogical Register, Vol. 41, p. 409.
  17. Frederick Clifton Pierce.

EPHRAIM HILDRETH.—Of Dracut. Served 21 weeks in Capt. Eleazer Tyng's Company in 1725.

REFERENCE: Massachusetts Archives, Vol. 61, p. 196.
  2. Captain Philip Reade.

LIEUTENANT   JAMES   HILDRETH.—[1631-1695]—Of Chelmsford, Mass. Was Lieutenant in the Military Company.

REFERENCE: Middlesex Probate Records; Cambridge Probate Records, 1695.
  2. Captain Philip Reade.

SERGEANT RICHARD HILDRETH.—[1605-1688]—Of Woburn. Prior to March 3, 1663, he was Sergeant in the Military Company at Chelmsford and served as such until 1664.

REFERENCE: Vol. 4, part 2, p. 100, Oct. 12, 1669, Gen. Court of the Colony of Mass. Bay in New England; History of Chelmsford.
  2. Captain Philip Reade.

SAMUEL HINCKLEY.—Was a member of Lieut. Thomas Dimmock's (Dymock's) Company at Barnstable, Mass., Aug., 1643.

REFERENCE: Pierce's Colonial Lists, p. 73.

37. Frank Bassett Tobey.

GOVERNOR THOMAS HINCKLEY.—Deputy to Plymouth General Court, 1646; Assistant, 1658 to 1680; Commissioner of Plymouth Colony against King Philip, 1675-76; at Great Swamp Fight. Deputy Governor, 1680; Governor, 1681; Assistant of Province Massachusetts Bay.

REFERENCE: Society Colonial Wars Year Book, 1895, p. 235.

50. Albert Eugene Snow.

ANDREW HINMAN, SR.—Was commissioned Captain of South Company at Woodbury, Conn., on May 10, 1733.

REFERENCE: Hinman's Early Puritan Settlers; Connecticut Colonial Records, 1726-35, p. 431.

52. Hobart Chatfield Chatfield-Taylor.

SERGT. EDWARD HINMAN.—Of Stratford, Conn. Sergeant-at-Arms in the Life Guard of King Charles the First. Associated with Capt. John Underhill in offering military service to Governor Stuyvesant against the Indians.

REFERENCE: Hinman's Genealogy of the Puritans.

56. Wyman Kneeland Flint.

TITUS HINMAN.—Was commissioned Lieutenant at Woodbury, Conn., on May 11, 1710; was promoted Captain May 13, 1714.

REFERENCE: Hinman's Early Puritan Settlers; Connecticut Colonial Records, 1706-16, p. 143-426.

52. Hobart Chatfield Chatfield-Taylor.

CAPTAIN LUKE HITCHCOCK, JR.—[1655-1727]—Soldier in King Philip's War. He served under Captain Turner in the Falls fight, May, 1676.

REFERENCE: N. E. Hist. and Gen. Register, Vol. 40, p. 212; Bates' Address in Westfield Centennial, p. 66; Hitchcock Family, p. 407-408-410; West Springfield Centennial; Mason A. Greene's History of Springfield, p. 166-193; Holland's History of Western Massachusetts, Vol. 2, p. 318; Chapin family, p. 292.

68. Albert Judson Fisher.

CAPTAIN LUKE HITCHCOCK, SR.—[—— 1659]—Of Wethersfield, Conn., 1644; soldier and Captain in early Colonial wars.

REFERENCE: Savage's Genealogical Dictionary; American Ancestry; History of Hitchcock Family, p. 205-206.

68. Albert Judson Fisher.

THOMAS HOLBROOK.—(1624-1697.) Of Braintree, Mass. Was a soldier in Capt. Johnson's Company.

REFERENCES: Soldiers in King Philip's War, by G. M. Bodge, pp. 162, 447; Mass. Archives, Vol. 67, p. 293.

74. Hiram Holbrook Rose.
91. Landon Cabell Rose.

RANDALL HOLDEN.—Was Marshal and Corporal at Portsmouth, R. I., 1638; was member of Town Council of Warwick, R. I., 1647; was Assistant of the Colony, 1647-53 to 1658-64-5-76; Deputy to General Court of R. I. ten years during the period 1666-86; was Judge of the Court of Common Pleas, 1687-8; was called Captain in Col. Records, Oct 26, 1664.

REFERENCE: Austin's Genealogical Dictionary of R. I.; Savage's Genealogical Dictionary, Vol. 2, p. 445; R. I. Colonial Records, Vol 2 (1664-77), p. 22-37-61-72-91-150-39.

75. Warren Lippitt Beckwith.

LIEUTENANT JOHN HOLLISTER.—[1612-1665]—Of Wethersfield, Conn.; a Deputy to the General Court, 1644, and many times thereafter, till 1656; member of the Wethersfield Train Band.

REFERENCE: Society of Colonial Wars Year Book, 1891, p. 55.

1. Seymour Morris.

CAPTAIN STEPHEN HOLLISTER.—[1658-1709]—Of Wethersfield, Conn.; member of the Wethersfield Train Band.

REFERENCE:—History of Waterbury, Conn.

1. Seymour Morris.

JOSHUA HOLMES.—Was Ensign in Connecticut Colonial forces at Stonington, Conn. He was appointed Oct., 1729.

REFERENCE: Connecticut Colonial Records, Vol. 1726-1735, p. 262.

10. Edward Milton Adams.
51. Franklin Adams Meacham.

GILES HOPKINS.—Volunteered for campaign against Pequot Indians, June 7, 1637.

REFERENCE: Plymouth Colony Records; Pierce's Colonial
Lists, p. 84.

58. Frederick Laforrest Merrick.
63. Rev. Abbott Eliot Kittredge.

LIEUTENANT JOHN HOPKINS.—[1660-1732]—Of Waterbury, Conn.; Sergeant, 1714; Ensign, 1715; Lieutenant, 1716.

REFERENCE: History of Waterbury, Conn., p. 152.
1. Seymour Morris.

STEPHEN HOPKINS.—Came in the Mayflower, 1620, a
member of Capt. Myles Standish's Military Company, which
was formed February, 1621. In summer of 1621 sent by Gov.
Bradford with Edw. Winslow (afterward Governor) on a historic mission to King Massasoit. In 1633-36, a member of the
Governor's Council; 1637, volunteered to go with other members of Colony to aid Massachusetts Bay and Connecticut Colonies in their war with the Pequots. In 1642, chosen one of a
Council of War for Plymouth.

REFERENCE: Davis' Ancient Landmarks of Plymouth; New
England Historical and Genealogical Register, Vol. 47, p. 81-83-186-
187; Vol. 22, p. 60-63-191; Morton's memoranda, p. 68-74; Society of
Colonial Wars Year Book, 1895, p. 236.

15. Josiah Lewis Lombard.
18. Scott Jordan.
50. Albert Eugene Snow.
58. Frederick Laforrest Merrick.
63. Rev. Abbott Eliot Kittredge.

WILLIAM HOPKINS.—Assistant Governor, 1641-2.

REFERENCE: Savage's Genealogical Dictionary.
42. Charles Thomson Atkinson.
64. Harry Jenkins Bardwell.

SERGEANT WILLIAM HOUGH.—Of Gloucester, Mass., and
New London, Conn. Was Sergeant of the first Military Company of New London. Member of committee on fortifications.

REFERENCE: Savage's Genealogical Dictionary of N. E.;
Caulkin's History of New London, Conn., p. 183-300; Babson's History of Gloucester, Mass., p. 105; Connecticut Colonial Records, Vol.
3, p. 241.

68. Albert Judson Fisher.
96. Oliver Partridge Dickinson.

HENRY HOUGHTON.—Soldier in the garrison commanded by Josiah Whitcomb at Lancaster during Queen Anne's War, 1704, composed of those who lived in Bolton, toward the northeast corner. Was himself in command of a garrison at Lancaster.

REFERENCE: Nourse's "Military Annals of Lancaster," p. 133; Nourse's "Early Records of Lancaster," p. 143-173; Mass Archives, Vol. 71, p. 876; Marvin's "History of Lancaster," p. 110.

68. Albert Judson Fisher.

JOHN HOUGHTON, JR.—[1650-1737]—Town Clerk of Lancaster from 1686 to 1725; soldier in garrison of Lawrence Waters at Lancaster in King Philip's War, 1676, and in garrison of Capt. Thos. Wilder in 1704. He had a garrison house in 1711. Was Magistrate; Representative to the General Court fourteen years, between 1693 and 1724.

REFERENCE: Nourse's "Early Records of Lancaster," p. 173-339; Willard's "Centennial Address," p. 95; Marvin's "History of Lancaster," p. 110-144-668-669-739-740; Mass. Archives, Vol. 71, p. 876; "American Ancestry," Vol. 9, p. 113.

68. Albert Judson Fisher.

JOHN HOUGHTON, SR.—At Lancaster, Mass., 1653-1684. During King Philip's War, after second Indian attack upon Lancaster, Feb. 10, 1676, he served in the Lawrence Waters garrison on the east side of North River.

REFERENCE: Willard's "Centennial Address," p. 95; Marvin's "History of Lancaster," p. 110-149-729-740; "American Ancestry," Vol. 9, p. 113.

68. Albert Judson Fisher.

THOMAS HOVEY.—[1648-1739]—Of Hadley. Lieutenant in King Philip's War.

REFERENCE: Savage's Genealogical Dictionary.

43. Harry Linn Wright.

JOHN HOW.—[—— 1687]—Sudbury, Mass., in 1638. Soldier in King Philip's War; in garrison in 1675.

REFERENCE: Society of Colonial Wars Year Book; Hudson's "History of Marlborough," p. 380-381; Hudson's "Annals of Sudbury, Wayland and Maynard," p. 22-253; Savage's Gen. Dictionary.

68. Albert Judson Fisher.
99. Eames Mac Veagh.

ISAAC HOWE.—Was appointed Ensign of First Company, or Train Band, at Stamford, Conn., in Oct., 1722; was also Ensign in 1732.

REFERENCE: Conn. Colonial Records, p. 331; Huntington Hist. Stamford, Conn., p. 185.

10.   Edward Milton Adams.

JOSIAH HOWE, SR.—[—— 1711]—In Marlborough, Mass., in 1675, and "rallied with others to defend the inhabitants at the opening of King Philip's War."

REFERENCE: Hudson's "History of Marlborough," p. 380-381-385; Hudson's "Annals of Sudbury, Wayland and Maynard," Ed. 1891, p. 253.

68.   Albert Judson Fisher.

EDWARD HOWELL.—[1585-1656]—Lynn, Mass.   Assistant 1647-53, Connecticut Colony.

REFERENCE: Society Colonial Wars Year Book, 1895.

42.   Charles Thomson Atkinson.

MAJOR JOHN HOWELL.—[1625-1695]—Southampton, L. I. Deputy, 1662-64.   Commander Troop of Horse, 1684.

REFERENCE: Society Colonial Wars Year Book, 1895.

42.   Charles Thomson Atkinson.

THOMAS HOWES, SR.—Was a member of Capt. William Palmer's Military Company at Yarmouth, Mass., Aug., 1643.

REFERENCE: Pierce's Colonial Lists, p. 74.

37.   Frank Bassett Tobey.

THOMAS HOWES, JR.—[—— 1676]—Was Ensign at Yarmouth, Mass., 1672 to 1674; was promoted Captain June 3, 1674; was member of War Council, which controlled garrison at Yarmouth, Mass.   Appointed April 2, 1667.

REFERENCE: Plymouth Col. Records, Vol. 5, p. 92-113-143-146-164-195-134.

37.   Frank Bassett Tobey.

JOHN HOWLAND.—[1593-1673]—Signer of Compact on the Mayflower. He was Assistant in Plymouth Colony, 1633-45, and as late as 1670 was serving as Deputy from Plymouth. Assistant to the Governor to raise soldiers, 1637.

REFERENCE: Year Book, Society of Colonial Wars; Savage's Genealogical Dictionary; Davis' Ancient Landmarks of Plymouth.

4. William Ruggles Tucker.
5. John Smith Sargent.
10. Edward Milton Adams.
51. Franklin Adams Meacham.
93. Wyllys King Smith.
105. Henry Clay Fuller.

JOHN HOWLAND, JR.—(1627 ——.) Ensign of the military company of Barnstable, Mass., in King Philip's War.

REFERENCES: Year Book Nat. Soc. of Col. Wars, 1896; Soldiers in King Philip's War, by Bodge, p. 439.

105. Henry Clay Fuller.

THOMAS HUCKINS.—Of Barnstable. Member of Colonial War Council, June 5, 1671, to inaugurate campaign against Awashonk, the Squaw Sachem; was Commissary General of all Plymouth Colony forces in King Philip's War, 1675; was member of Barnstable Town War Council, Feb. 29, 1675.

REFERENCE: Pierce's Colonial Lists, p. 94-96-98; Plymouth Colonial Records; Society of Colonial Wars Year Book, 1895.

50. Albert Eugene Snow.

DANIEL HUDSON.—[1697]—Of Lancaster. Soldier in Capt. Joseph Sill's Company, King Philip's War; also in garrison at Lancaster, 1691-2.

REFERENCE: N. E. Hist. and Gen. Reg., Vol. 41, p. 407; Vol. 43, p. 261.

18. Scott Jordan.

LIEUTENANT CORNELIUS HULL.—Fairfield, Conn; messenger of the Council of War, Oct., 1675; appointed Lieutenant of the "Honored Major Treat's Life Guard," 1675, King Philip's War; Deputy from Fairfield to the General Court, 1676.

REFERENCE: Society of Colonial Wars Year Book, 1895, p. 238-239; Connecticut Colonial Records, Vol. 1665-1677, p. 411-378-279-327; also Vol. 1689-1706, p. 507; Vol. 1706-1716, p. 109-115-130.

48. Henry Austin Osborn.

CAPTAIN THEOPHILUS HULL.—Ensign, 1705; Lieutenant, 1709; Captain, 1709, of the West Military Company of Fairfield, Conn.; member of the "Committee of War," Fairfield County, 1709.

REFERENCE: Society of Colonial Wars Year Book, 1895, p. 238-239; Connecticut Colonial Records, Vol. 1665-1677, p. 411-373-279-327; also Vol. 1689-1706, p. 507; 1706-1716, p. 109-115-130.

48. Henry Austin Osborn.

SERGEANT JOHN HUMPHREY.—Was Sergeant in the Simsbury, Conn., Train Band. Simsbury, Conn., town records call him "Sergt.," Dec. 20, 1693.

REFERENCE: Simsbury Probate Records, Vol. 2, p 48; Simsbury Town Records (manuscript). Humphrey Genealogy, by F. Humphreys.

10. Edward Milton Adams.
33. Deming Haven Preston.

LIEUTENANT SAMUEL HUMPHREY.—Was Ensign, 1698; was Lieutenant, 1710; was Deputy from Simsbury, 1702, and later. Commissioned Lieutenant by Gov. Saltonstall, May, 1710.

REFERENCE: Mass. and Conn. Colonial Records; Humphrey Genealogy, by F. Humphrey.

10. Edward Milton Adams.
72. Lester Orestes Goddard.

EPHRAIM HUNT, JR.—Was Captain in the expedition to the St. Lawrence River, under Sir William Phipps in 1690; was given title for services then rendered, of Colonel. In expedition against Indians at Groton in 1706-7. He was also Governor's Councillor, or Assistant, from 1703 until his death in 1713. Appointed Ensign at Weymouth, Mass., March 16, 1680.

REFERENCE: Savage's Genealogical Dictionary; Ellis Genealogy, notes; History of Easton; Col. Records, 1674-86, p. 306; Pope Genealogy, p. 285.

44. James Monroe Flower.

SAMUEL HUNT, JR.—[1657-1742-3]—Of Concord, Billerica and Tewksbury, Mass. Soldier in Capt. John Lane's Company of Militia, Major Jonathan Tyng's regiment, 1702, and participated in the march and rescue to the relief of Lancaster, Mass., against the French and Indians. His home near Wameset, now called Lowell, Mass., was used as a garrison during King William's War, 1689-1697, and also during Queen Anne's War, 1700-1712.

REFERENCE: History of Billerica, Mass., p. 75-76, Genealogical Register of Billerica; report of Lieut.-Col. Jos. Lynde, dated Charlestown, Mass., Aug. 25, 1695; Court Records, Vol. 20, p. 444, and Vol. 16, p. 67; History of Connecticut Valley in Massachusetts, Vol. 2, Franklin Co., p. 687-688.

2. Captain Philip Reade.

SAMUEL HUNT, SR.—[1633 ——]—of Agawam, now called Ipswich, Mass., in 1655, then of Billerica, Mass. Was a grantee of Bernardstown, Franklin Co., Mass., in reward of military service in the Falls Fight, also Deerfield, Mass., May 19, 1676. He was a soldier in Capt. William Turner's Company of Volunteers in King Philip's War. He was also a soldier under Maj. Samuel Appleton against the Narragansetts and participated in the Great Swamp Fight, Dec. 19, 1675.

REFERENCE: Savage's Genealogical Dictionary, Vol. 2, p. 502; History of Ipswich, Mass., p. 147-323; History of Billerica, Mass., p. 117-133-137.

2. Captain Philip Reade.

WILLIAM HUNT.—[1605-1667]—Soldier in Capt. William Turner's Troop of Dorchester and Boston, April 7, 1676.

REFERENCE: Mass. Archives, Vol. 68, p. 21-195.

2. Captain Philip Reade.

AMOS HURD.—He was a soldier in the old French wars called the Seven Years' War and perished of starvation in the campaign of 1759.

REFERENCE: Cothrens History of Ancient Woodbury; Society of Colonial Wars Register, 1894, p. 193.

23. Alfred Beers Eaton.

JONATHAN HYDE.—Was in Capt. Thomas Wheeler's Co., scouting near Sudbury and Marlboro, King Philip's War. His name appears on roll, June 24, 1676.

REFERENCE: N. E. Hist. and Gen. Reg. Vol. 38, p. 42.

52. Hobart Chatfield Chatfield-Taylor.

CAPT. WILLIAM HYDE.—(1702-1738.) In May, 1727, was appointed Captain of the Train Band at Norwich, Conn., by the General Assembly.

REFERENCES: Biographical Sketches Yale Graduates, class 1721, p. 257; also Caulkin's History of Norwich, 2nd edition, p. 188.

93. Wyllys King Smith.

GIDEON IVES.—(1680-1767.) Ensign of the east Train Band of Wallingford, Conn. Deputy 1720-21-23-24-29-31 and 49.

REFERENCES: Conn. Col. Records, 1717 to 1725, pp. 207, 233, 269, 304-311; Vol. 7, pp. 251, 267, 346, 363 and 424; Vol. 9, pp. 318, 348, 413 and 460; Davis' History of Wallingford and Meriden, pp. 823 to 829.

102. Marvin Allen Ives.

JOHN JENNEY.—Of Plymouth, was "Assistant" of Plymouth Colony, 1637-8-1640.

REFERENCE: Plymouth Colonial Records; Pierce's Colonial Lists, p. 4.

50. Albert Eugene Snow.

EDWARD JOHNSON.—Was Captain of Woburn, Mass., Militia Company; charter member of A. & H. Artillery Company, Boston; Surveyor General of Arms for Mass., 1659; Deputy thirty times.

REFERENCE: Society of Colonial Wars Year Book, 1894, p. 126-185; Savage's Gen. Dict.

10. Edward Milton Adams.
51. Franklin Adams Meacham.

CAPTAIN ISAAC JOHNSON.—[—— 1675]—A member of the Artillery Company in 1645. Ensign of the Roxbury Military Company previous to 1653. Elected June 13, 1653, Captain of said company. Captain of Artillery Company in 1667. Representative to the General Court, 1671. Upon the mustering of the forces for Narragansett campaign he was placed in command of a company made up of men from Roxbury, Dorchester, Milton, Braintree, Weymouth, Hingham and Hull. Killed while leading his men across the fatal tree bridge at the entrance to the fort, Dec. 19, 1675.

REFERENCE: N. E. H. and G. Reg., Vol. 38, p. 280; Vol. 39, p. 74; Massachusetts Archives, Vol. 67, p. 45-219-226-293; Society of Colonial Wars Year Book, 1894, p. 39.

1. Seymour Morris.
47. Maj. Forrest Henry Hathaway, U. S. A.

JOHN JOHNSON.—[1600-1659]—Of Roxbury. A member of the first General Court in 1634, and for many years thereafter; a member of the Artillery Company in 1638; Surveyor General of arms and ammunition.

REFERENCE: Society of Colonial Wars Year Book, 1894, p. 39; Savage's Gen. Dict.; Mass. Bay Colonial Records, Vol. 1, p. 79; Vol. 2, p. 22-26-55-99-145-186-197-201-238-245-265; Vol. 4, part 1, p. 2-37-74-77-110-120-154-255-286-304-320-365.

1. Seymour Morris.
47. Maj. Forrest Henry Hathaway, U. S. A.
68. Albert Judson Fisher.
82. Marvin Andrus Farr.

ANDREW JOHNSTONE.—[1694-1762]—Of Perth Amboy, N. J. Speaker of Provincial Assembly; for many years a member of the Governor's Council.

REFERENCE: Lamb's History of New York City; Appleton's Cyclopedia of American Biography; History of Trenton, N. J.; American Historical Register, Vol. 1, p. 1-2.

4. William Ruggles Tucker.

NATHANIEL JONES.—Captain.   Representative to the General Court of Suffolk County, Mass., in 1727.

REFERENCE: Bond's History of Watertown; Reminiscences of Worcester, Mass.; Proprietary Records of Worcester, p. 283-261-251-244.

5. John Smith Sargent.

JOHN JORDAN.—A member of the Plymouth Company in August, 1643.

REFERENCE: Pierce's Plymouth Colony Civil & Mil. Lists, p. 76; Plymouth Colony Records.

61. Victor Clifton Alderson.

SAMUEL JORDAN.—Of "Seven Islands," Buckingham County, Virginia. Was Justice of the Peace 1746-1761; Sheriff 1753-5; one of the trustees for erecting a blast furnace for making pig iron (for molding cannon) in the county of Buckingham, Virginia; Captain, 1753; Presiding Justice and County Lieutenant for Buckingham County, 1761; was appointed by the Assembly of Virginia one of the Commissioners to examine the militia accounts in 1758.

REFERENCES: Hennings' Statutes at Large, Vol. 7. pp. 232; Cabells and Their Kin, A. Brown, pp. 49, 78, 104, 127 and 128.

74. Hiram Holbrook Rose.
91. Landon Cabell Rose.

JOHN JUDD.—Ensign and Lieutenant, Farmington Train Band; Deputy from Farmington.

REFERENCE: Colonial Records of Connecticut, 1689-1706; p. 65-75-79-89, etc., p. 142-235-245-264-434.

42. Charles Thomson Atkinson.

LIEUT. JOSEPH JUDSON.—Ensign of the Stratford Train Band. Lieutenant in 1672, and at Woodbury in 1684. On July 6, 1665, appointed by the General Court as one of a committee to defend the coast from Stratford to Rye against a threatened invasion of the Dutch, under Admiral De Reuter, Deputy, 1659-61 to '67, from Stratford, and Deputy for Woodbury, 1684 to 6. Served in King Philip's War with the rank of Lieutenant.

REFERENCES: Conn. Col. Records, Vol. 1; Vol. 2, pp. 21 and 181; Vol. 3, p. 141; Bodge's Soldiers in King Philip's War, p. 468.

101. John Newbury Bagley.

SAMUEL KEELER.—Of Norwalk, Conn. Was in the Narragansett fight in King Philip's war, December 19, 1675. Representative 1701. Commissioned Lieutenant in the expedition against Port Royal August 11, 1710. Received £5 18s 2d for actual services rendered.

REFERENCES: Savage's Gen. Dict., Vol. 3, p. 2; Conn. Col. Records, Vol. 1706-1716, pp. 168 and 264.
48. Henry Austin Osborn.
64. Harry Jenkins Bardwell.

LIEUTENANT JOSEPH KELLOGG.—Of Farmington, Conn., Boston, and Hadley, Mass.; was Lieutenant in command of Hadley, Mass., troops in the Falls Fight, May 18, 1676. Sergeant in Capt. Wm. Turner's Company in the Falls Fight, May 19, 1676.

REFERENCE: Judd's History of Hadley, Mass.; Savage's Genealogical Dictionary; Society of Colonial Wars Year Book, 1895, p. 242.
10. Edward Milton Adams.
21. William Wolcott Strong.
43. Harry Linn Wright.

HENRY KIMBALL.—Member of the quota of soldiers furnished by the Town of Haverhill, Mass., Bay Colony.

REFERENCE: History of Haverhill, p. 128.
2. Captain Philip Reade.

JOHN KITTREDGE.—(——1676.) Of Billerica, Mass., a member of Captain Thomas Wheeler's Company in King Philip's War.

REFERENCE: Soldiers in King Philip's War, by Bodge, pages 113 and 114.
63. Rev. Abbott Eliot Kittredge.

EDWARD KNEELAND.—Born 1640. Was in Capt. Whipple's Ipswich Company in King Philip's War.

REFERENCES: Pay Rolls of June and August, 1676; Bodge's Soldiers in King Philip's War.
56. Wyman Kneeland Flint.

SAMUEL LADD.—(1649-1698.) Of Haverhill, Mass. A member of Capt. John Whipple's Company in King Philip's War.

REFERENCE: Bodge's Soldiers in King Philip's War, pp. 283, 372.
88. Edward Payson Bailey.

ENSIGN JOHN LAKIN.—[—— 1697]—Ensign, 1692. Commander of garrison at Groton. Sergeant in King Philip's War.

REFERENCE: Society of Colonial Wars Year Book, 1895, p. 213.

26. Horatio Loomis Wait.

MAJOR JOB LANE.—[1624-1697]—Malden, Mass., 1654. Billerica, 1664. During King Philip's War had a garrison against Indians. Representative to General Court, 1674, 1680 and 1685.

REFERENCE: Society of Colonial Wars Year Book; Hazen's "History of Billerica," p. 88 of Appendix 3, 139-176; Mass. Bay Colonial Records, Vol. 3, p. 99-261-393-476; the Reyner family; the Lane family.

45. Francis Porter Fisher.

68. Albert Judson Fisher.

70. Charles Ridgely.

COLONEL JOHN LANE.—[1661-1715]—Lieutenant of the Billerica Troop, 1693, King William's War. Captain of the same, 1699. Major of the West Regiment of Horse and Foot, 1711, Queen Anne's War. Deputy to the General Court, 1702. Colonel of Massachusetts Militia. Died in the service.

REFERENCE: S. C. W. Year Book, 1895, p. 243.

73. Anthony French Merrill.

CAPT. JOSEPH LATHROP.—(1624-1702.) A Deputy from Barnstable in 1667 and for eleven consecutive years following; a conspicuous member of the "Council of War" in 1676; member of the Barnstable Military Company in 1643, and later Lieutenant and Captain. Mentioned to the Governor for conspicuous services in the Indian Wars.

REFERENCES: Freeman's Cape Cod, Vol. 1, pp. 295, 300, 311, 382; Pierce's Colonial Lists, p. 73; Savage, Vol. 3, p. 121; Lathrop Family Memoir, p. 40.

64. Harry Jenkins Bardwell.

THOMAS LATHROP.—(1621-1707.) Barnstable. A member of the Barnstable Military Company in 1643.

REFERENCE: Pierce's Colonial Lists, p. 73.

64. Harry Jenkins Bardwell.

CAPTAIN DANIEL LAWRENCE.—[1681-1777]—Of Groton, Mass., and Plainfield, Conn., May, 1736. Commissioned Captain of the First Company or Train Band of Plainfield, Conn.; was Deputy from Plainfield to General Court eleven times between 1722 and 1741.

REFERENCE: Colonial Records of Connecticut, Vol. 8, p. 32; Dr. R. M. Lawrence's "Historical Sketches of the Lawrence Family," p. 42-43.

18. Scott Jordan.

ENOCH LAWRENCE.—[1648-9-1744]—Of Watertown and Groton. A soldier in King Philip's War; also in Groton Garrison, 1691-2; was badly wounded in a fight with Indians, July 27, 1694, King William's War.

REFERENCE: N. E. Hist. and Gen. Reg., Vol. 43, p. 274-374; Dr. S. A. Greene's "Groton During the Indian Wars," p. 84-85; Historical Sketches of the Lawrence family, p. 38-39; Massachusetts Archives, Vol. 70, p. 683.

18. Scott Jordan.

ROBERT LEE.—A member of the Plymouth Military Company in August, 1643.

REFERENCE: Pierce's Colonial List, p. 76.

105. Henry Clay Fuller.

LIEUT. THOMAS LEE.—1676, Deputy to the General Court; 1701, Ensign and Lieutenant of Lyme Train Band.

REFERENCE: S. C. W. Year Book, 1896, p. 348.

71. Ebenezer Lane.

ENSIGN THOMAS LEE.—Ensign of the Lyme Train Band, 1701; Deputy to the General Court, 1676, of the Colony of Connecticut.

REFERENCE: Society of Colonial Wars Year Book, 1895, p. 24.

71. Ebenezer Lane.

GOVERNOR WILLIAM LEETE.—Governor of Connecticut, 1661 to 1665, and again, 1677 to 1683; was Assistant, 1669 and 1643 to 1657. Deputy Governor, 1658-76; was Commissioner to United Colonies, 1655 to 1679.

REFERENCE: Society of Colonial Wars Year Book, 1894, p. 42.

10. Edward Milton Adams.

ENSIGN THOMAS LEFFINGWELL.—Ensign in 1701 in the Norwich, Conn., Train Band; Deputy, 1716.

REFERENCE: Conn. Col. Records, Vol. 3.

70. Charles Ridgely.

71. Ebenezer Lane.

LIEUTENANT THOMAS LEFFINGWELL.—Ensign in 1657; Lieutenant of the Norwich County Train Band, 1672; served in King Philip's War; also served in Capt. Denison's famous band of Indian fighters. Deputy to the General Court, 1671-1710.

REFERENCE: Society of Colonial Wars Year Book, 1895, p. 245.

70. Charles Ridgely.

71. Ebenezer Lane.

JOHN LEONARD—Of Springfield, Mass., 1639. He was killed by the Indians in King Philip's War early in 1676.

REFERENCE: Savage's Gen. Dict.; Judd's History of Hadley, Mass.; N. E. Hist. and Gen. Register, Vol. 40, p. 212; History of W. Mass., Vol. 2, p. 318.

  60. John Conant Long.
  68. Albert Judson Fisher.
  96. Oliver Partridge Dickinson.

LIEUTENANT JAMES LEWIS.—[1637-1713]—Lieutenant of Barnstable Company.

REFERENCE: Society of Colonial Wars Year Book, 1895, p. 246.

  15. Josiah Lewis Lombard.

SAMUEL LEWIS.—Was Sergeant. Farmington, Conn., 1676.

REFERENCE: Savage's Genealogical Dictionary, N. E.

  42. Charles Thomson Atkinson.

CAPTAIN WILLIAM LEWIS.—A Sergeant and Captain in the Narragansett campaign, King Philip's War, 1675; Sergeant, May 17, 1649; Lieutenant, Oct. 6, 1651; Captain, Oct. 8, 1674. Captain of the Farmington, Conn., Train Band in 1674; Deputy, 1689-90.

REFERENCE: Savage's Genealogical Dictionary of New England, Vol. III, p. 89; Connecticut Colonial Records, Vol. 1636-1665, pp. 187, 227, 300. Vol. 1665, 1677, pp. 101 and 238. Society of Colonial Wars Year Book, 1895, p. 246.

  33. Deming Haven Preston.
  42. Charles Thomson Atkinson.
  59. Charles Pratt Whitney.
  64. Harry Jenkins Bardwell.

ROBERT LONG.—Charlestown, Mass.; a member of the Ancient and Honorable Artillery Company, of Boston, 1639.

REFERENCE: Savage's Genealogical Dictionary.

   1. Seymour Morris.
  28. Cyrus Austin Hardy.
  52. Hobart Chatfield Chatfield-Taylor.

CAPT. MATTHEW LOOMIS.—(1703-1764.) Appointed Ensign, 1752; First Lieutenant in Regiment raised for invasion of Canada, 1758; Captain, 1761, in Company from Bolton, Conn.

REFERENCES: Conn. Col. Records, Vol. 10, p. 81; Vol. 11, pp. 96 and 575.

  96. Oliver Partridge Dickinson.

CAPTAIN RICHARD LORD.—[1611-1662]—Was Captain of the First Troop of Horse, Colony of Conn., 1657. One of the patentees under the charter of 1662 from Charles II.

REFERENCE: Society of Colonial Wars Year Book, 1895, p. 248.

7. Edward McKinstry Teall.

LIEUTENANT RICHARD LORD.—[1669-1712]—Was Treasurer of the Colony of Connecticut, elected Jan. 14, 1712. He was elected Auditor, 1706; Lieutenant, May, 1700; on Committee on War, 1708.

REFERENCE: Connecticut Colonial Records for 1689 to 1716.

7. Edward McKinstry Teall.

CAPTAIN EBENEZER LOTHROP.—Commissioned Ensign in First Train Band, Norwich, Conn., 1740; Lieutenant in 1742; Captain in 1745.

REFERENCE: Connecticut Colonial Records.

70. Charles Ridgely.

CAPT. ELISHA LOTHROP.—Was Ensign and Captain of the Sixth Company of Connecticut Colonial Troops, in 1746. Deputy in 1766 and many times thereafter.

REFERENCES: Conn. Col. Records, Vol. 8, p. 226; Vol. 9, p. 241; Vol. 13.

70. Charles Ridgely.

CAPTAIN SAMUEL LOTHROP.—Served at Port Royal in 1710. Commissioned Ensign in 1721, Fourth Train Band of Connecticut; in 1724 commissioned Captain of Second Train Band.

REFERENCE: Colonial Records, Vol. 3, pp. 235-446.

70. Charles Ridgely.

JUDGE SAMUEL LOTHROP.—When, in 1657, Uncas routed by the Narragansetts, had been chased into the fort at the head of the Nahantic and was there besieged, Lieut. James Avery, Mr. Brewster, Samuel Lothrop and others succeeded in throwing themselves into the fort and aided in the defense.

REFERENCE: Lothrop Family Memoir.

65. Joseph Lathrop.
70. Charles Ridgely.
102. Marvin Allen Ives.

DANIEL LOVETT.—Was Lieutenant, 1730; Captain, 1735; Major, 1743, at Mendon, Mass.

REFERENCE: See Annals of Mendon, copying town records, pp. 216, 227, 246, 253.

10. Edward Milton Adams.
51. Franklin Adams Meacham.

JAMES LOVETT.—Of Mendon, Mass. Was Sergeant, 1689; Ensign, 1693; Lieutenant, 1710; Captain later.

REFERENCE: Annals of Mendon, copying town records, pp. 106, 117, 121, 159 and later.

10. Edward Milton Adams.
51. Franklin Adams Meacham.

MAJ. ANTHONY LOW.—(Died 1752.)   Rhode Island Militia, 1726. Deputy, 1713, sixteen terms.

REFERENCE: S. C. W. Year Book, 1896, p. 353.

75. Warren Lippitt Beckwith.

WILLIAM LUMPKIN.—A private in the Yarmouth, Mass., Company.

REFERENCE: Pierce's Colonial Lists, p. 74.

15. Josiah Lewis Lombard.
32. Rev. James Gibson Johnson.
63. Rev. Abbott Eliot Kittredge.

FRANCIS LYFORD.—[1645-1723]—A private in Capt. Kinsley Hall's Company of Exeter, N. H., in King William's War.

REFERENCE: Bell's History of Exeter, N. H.

39. George Samuel Marsh.

LIEUTENANT JOHN LYMAN.—He was in command of the Northampton soldiers in the famous Falls Fight above Deerfield, May 18, 1676. Capt. William Turner, under whom he served, was killed.

REFERENCE: Lyman Genealogy, p. 40. New England Historical and Genealogical Register, Vol. 41, pp. 201 to 218.

6. Lyman Dresser Hammond.
54. William Ward Wight.

HON. SIMON LYNDE.—(1624-1687.) Services: Ancient and Honorable Artillery Company, 1658; Governor's Assistant, 1668-1679; King Philip's War, 1675; Chief Justice Supreme Court, 1687.

REFERENCES: General Society Year Book, 1895, p. 354; Col. Records, Mass. Bay Colony; Bodge's Soldiers of King Philip's War, p. 177.

78. Joseph Edward Otis, Jr.
81. George Henry Moore.
98. Philo Adams Otis.

CAPT. JABEZ LYON.—(1704-1760.) Woodstock, Conn. Was a Captain of the Third Company or Train Band, October, 1750.

REFERENCES: Conn. Col. Records, Vol. 9, p. 550; Albert Welles' American Family Antiquity, New York, 1881, Vol. 2, p. 107.

40. Chandler Pease Chapman.

WILLIAM LYON.—(1620-1692.) Roxbury, Mass. In 1645 was member of the Ancient and Honorable Artillery Company.

REFERENCES: Albert Welles' American Family Antiquity, New York, 1881, Vol. 2, p. 105; An Historical Sketch of the Ancient and Honorable Artillery Co., Boston, 1820, p. 155.

40. Chandler Pease Chapman.

WILLIAM LYON.—(1729-1809.) He entered the Provincial Military service from Carlisle, Penn., for the defense of the frontier against the French and Indians, and as Lieutenant of the Pennsylvania Regiment, appointed 6th of December, 1757, participated in Forbes' great expedition against Fort Du Quesne in 1758. He resigned March 1759, and was appointed a Magistrate in 1764 by Governor John Penn, then in Carlisle, Pa., dispatching Colonel Bouquet on his second expedition.

REFERENCE: Dr. Wm. Henry Egle's Penn. Genealogies, Scotch, Irish and German, pp. 334 and 335.

106. George Mulhollan Lyon.

LIEUTENANT GEORGE MACEY.—Of Taunton. Ensign, ——. Promoted to Lieutenant, June, 1665; promoted Captain, April, 1690; made Associate Judge, June, 1690; was member of Capt. Poole's Co., of Taunton, 1643; was Lieutenant from Taunton, Mass., King Philip's War; Deputy Plymouth Colony, 1672-78.

REFERENCE: Plymouth Colony Records, Vol. IV, p. 93; Vol. VI, p. 237; Pierce's Colonial Lists, pp. 75; Savage's Gen. Dict.; Baylie's New Plymouth; Society of Colonial Wars Year Book, 1895.

45. Francis Porter Fisher.

JOHN MARSH.—(1679-1725.)   A soldier at the battle of
Deerfield Meadow in February, 1704, Queen Anne's War; taken
captive by the enemy and carried to Montreal.

REFERENCE: Sheldon's Deerfield, pp. 298, 305, 309.
64.   Harry Jenkins Bardwell.

ONESIPHOROUS MARSH, SR.—[1630-1713]—Of Haverhill,
Mass.   Member of the Militia Company under Capt. William
White, in 1662.   He was in command of and owned one of the
small garrison forts built by the town in King Philip's War,
1675.   During King William's War, 1684-1697, he was a member of one of the town garrisons, commanded by Sergeant Has-
eltine.

REFERENCE: Town Records, p. 117; Savage, Vol. III, p. 154;
History of Essex Co., Mass.; History of Haverhill; Sewall's Diary.
2.   Captain Philip Reade.

CAPTAIN HUGH MASON.—[1605-1678]—Of Watertown.
Deputy to the General Court of Mass. nine times, 1635-77. Com-
mander in Chief, 1664; member of the Council of War, 1676;
Lieutenant and Captain of the Train Band of Watertown,
Mass., 1652; in command of the Watertown Militia in the Sud-
bury fight, King Philip's War, April 21, 1676.

REFERENCE: Society of Colonial Wars Year Book, 1894, pp.
76, 174, 183, 189 and 210.
25.   Judge Frank Baker.

MAJOR JOHN MASON.—Lieutenant under Sir Thomas
Fairfax in the Netherlands; Representative to General Court,
1635-1641; Deputy Governor, 1659-1669; Commissioner to the
United Colonies for five sessions, 1647-1661; commanded forces
in Pequot War.

REFERENCE: Sparks' American Biography, Vol. III; Year
Book, 1894; Society of Colonial Wars, p. 47.
42.   Charles Thomson Atkinson.
64.   Harry Jenkins Bardwell.
99.   Eames Mac Veagh.

PHILIP MATTOON.—(——1696.)   Credited on December 10,
1675, with £2 10s 6d, under Capt. Samuel Appleton, and on
June 24, 1676, with £2 15s 08d.   Served in Narragansett Campaign.   Served under Capt. William Turner from April 7, 1676.

REFERENCES: Bodge's Soldiers 'n King Philip's War, pp.
154, 155, 157, 241; Mass. Archives, Vol. 68, p. 97.
89.   Albert Mattoon Graves.

JOHN MAYO.—A member of the "Barnstable Company" of Plymouth Colony, Lieutenant Thomas Dymoke commanding. Active service in 1643-44.

REFERENCE: Society of Colonial Wars Year Book, 1895, p. 253.

15. Josiah Lewis Lombard.
32. Rev. James Gibson Johnson.
63. Rev. Abbott Eliot Kittredge.

SAMUEL MAYO.—A member of the "Barnstable Company" of Plymouth Colony, Lieutenant Thomas Dymoke commanding. Active service in 1643-44.

REFERENCE: Society of Colonial Wars Year Book, 1895, p. 253; Pierce's Colonial Lists, p. 73.

15. Josiah Lewis Lombard.
32. Rev. James Gibson Johnson.
63. Rev. Abbott Eliot Kittredge.

LIEUTENANT JAMES M'DOWELL.—[1716 ——]—Of Augusta Co., Va. Was Lieutenant of an Augusta County, Va., company in the French and Indian War, 1754-63. Lieut. James McDowell, of Augusta County (Va.) Militia, received arrears of pay, by order of the General Assembly, Sept., 1758."

REFERENCE: Thos. Marshall Green's "Historic Families of Kentucky," 1st Series, pp. 12, 13; Hening's "Statutes at Large," Vol. VII, p. 195.

18. Scott Jordan.

JOHN MOHR M'INTOSH.—Settled at New Iverness, Ga. (now Darien) on the Albemarle. John Mohr McIntosh entered actively upon the defense of the Colony against the Spaniards. He was appointed Captain of a Highland company, the first in America. He was in command of this company during Gen. Oglethorpe's operations to capture St. Augustine from the Spaniards in 1740. He was the founder of McIntosh County and the County was named for him.

REFERENCE: Historical Register of Officers of the Continental Army, p. 278; Appleton's Cyclopedia of American Biography, Vol. 4, p. 124.

9. Frederick Hampden Winston.

CAPTAIN SAMUEL MEREDITH.—[1732-1808]—Captain in Col. Wm. Byrd's Regiment. Served at Forts Chiswell, Cumberland, Pitt, etc.

REFERENCE: Society of Colonial Wars Year Book, 1895, pp. 253-83 and 166.

74. Hiram Holbrook Rose.
91. Landon Cabell Rose.

WILLIAM MERRICK.—Was a member of the Duxbury Company of Plymouth Colony, under Capt. Myles Standish, in active service, 1642-1644. He was an Ensign at Eastham, Cape Cod, Mass. Was promoted to be Lieutenant, June, 1663.

REFERENCE: Pierce's Colonial Lists; Society Colonial Wars Year Book, 1895; Plymouth Colonial Records, Vol. IV, p. 41.

58. Frederick Laforrest Merrick.

NATHANIEL MERRIMAN.—Sergeant in Train Band at New Haven, on July —, 1665; promoted Lieutenant at Wallingford, Ct., May, 1672; promoted Captain of troop of dragoons for New Haven County, Nov. 1, 1675.

REFERENCE: Connecticut Colonial Records, Vol. 1665-1677, pp. 23, 172, 379.

59. Charles Pratt Whitney.
102. Marvin Allen Ives.

ELEAZER METCALF.—(1653-1706.) Ensign of the Wrentham Company, July 5, 1689.

REFERENCE: Mass. Archives; Court Record, Vol. 6, p. 59.

79. John Whipple Hill.

STEPHEN MIGHILL.—(1651——.) Of Rowley, Mass. Served in King Philip's War, 1675.

REFERENCE: S. C. W. Year Book, 1896, p. 359.

90. Edwin Fraser Gillette.

CAPT. JOHN MILES.—(1644-1704.) Served under Maj. Richard Treat in the Great Swamp Fight.

REFERENCE: S. C. W. Register, 1896, p. 359.

93. Wyllys King Smith.

CAPT. THOMAS MINER.—(1607-1690.) Deputy to the General Court, Massachusetts, 1665-70, 1673; Chief Military Officer at Mystick, Conn., 1665.

REFERENCE: S. C. W. 1896 Year Book, p. 359.

10. Edward Milton Adams.
51. Franklin Adams Meacham.
78. Joseph Edward Otis, Jr.
98. Philo Adams Otis.

CAPT. JAMES MINOTT.—(1653-1735.) Concord, Mass. Services: Captain Concord Militia Company, 1684; with expedition to Canada, 1690; Deputy to General Court, 1700-1701.

REFERENCES: Col. Records, Mass. Bay Colony; General Society Year Book for 1895, p. 254.
81. George Henry Moore.

EXPERIENCE MITCHELL.—A member of the Duxbury, Mass., Military Company, August, 1643.

REFERENCE: Pierce's Colonial Lists, p. 76.
90. Edwin Fraser Gillette.

ENSIGN JACOB MITCHELL.—Of Bridgewater, Mass. Killed King Philip's War, 1675.

REFERENCE: Mitchell's Bridgewater.
72. Lester Orestes Goddard.

LIEUTENANT JOHN MOFFETT.—[1708-1744]—Of Augusta Co., Va. "On June 24, 1742, John Moffett qualified as Lieutenant of Militia at the Orange County (Va.) Court."

REFERENCE: "Early Records of Orange Co. (Va.) Court," p. 396; Annals of Augusta Co., Va., 1853 Edition.
18. Scott Jordan.

WILLIAM MONROE.—[1669-1759]—Of Lexington. Ensign of Militia.

REFERENCE: Hudson History of Lexington, pp. 149.
25. Frank Baker.

ENSIGN JOHN MOORE.—[—— 1702]—Sudbury and Lancaster, Mass. Appointed Sergeant of Lancaster Company, April 20, 1670; elected its Ensign July 3, 1689; served in garrison at Lancaster, 1676, and after; Representative to the General Court, 1689-1690; Selectman, 1690. Died Sept., 1702.

REFERENCE: Nourse's "Military Annals of Lancaster," p. 9; Nourse's "Early Records of Lancaster," pp. 125, 128, 133; Marvin's "History of Lancaster," pp. 61-110; Willard's "Centennial Address," p. 95.
68. Albert Judson Fisher.

JOHN MOORE, SR.—[—— 1703]—Sudbury and Lancaster, Mass. At Sudbury, 1638, or earlier. Probably of Ancient and Honorable Artillery Co., 1638. Served in garrison of Lawrence Waters following the attack of King Philip's 1,500 warriors upon Lancaster, Feb. 10, 1676. Representative to the General Court, 1689 to 1692.

REFERENCE: Savage's Genealogical Dictionary; Hudson's "Annals of Sudbury, Wayland and Maynard," pp. 2, 201, 201; Marvin's "History of Lancaster," p. 110; Whitman's "History of A. & H. Artillery Co."; Willard's "Centennial Address," p. 95; Nourse's "Early Records of Lancaster," pp. 128, 333.

57.   Charles Clarence Poole.
68.   Albert Judson Fisher.

JONATHAN MOORE.—[1669-1742]—He and his brother John had a garrison during Queen Anne's War, 1704, at Lancaster, Mass.

REFERENCE: Nourse's "Early Records of Lancaster," pp. 143-306; Mass. Archives, LXXI, 876; Marvin's "History of Lancaster," pp. 110-138.

68.   Albert Judson Fisher.

DAVID MORGAN.—One of the defenders of Springfield, Mass., at its burning by the Indians during King Philip's War.

REFERENCE: History of Springfield, pp. 162, 165, by Mason A. Greene; Savage's Genealogical Dictionary; Morris' "Burning of Springfield"; Appendix, p. 74.

68.   Albert Judson Fisher.

CAPTAIN MILES MORGAN.—[1616-1699]—Of Springfield, Mass. An old Indian hunter. For many years Sergeant and afterward Captain of the military company of Springfield. Capt. Morgan built a block-house and stockade, which he and his five sons ably defended against the Indians.

REFERENCE: American Ancestry, Vol. 3, p. 36; History of Brimfield; History of Springfield, p. 126, by M. A. Greene.

68.   Albert Judson Fisher.

LIEUTENANT EDWARD MORRIS.—[1630-1689]—Of Roxbury, Mass., and Woodstock, Conn. Representative to the General Court from Roxbury, 1677-1687; founder of the town of Woodstock, Conn., in 1686, and their first military officer.

REFERENCE: Savage's Genealogical Dictionary; Year Book; Society of Colonial Wars; Larned's History of Windham County, Conn.

1.   Seymour Morris.
6.   Lyman Dresser Hammond.

LIEUTENANT EDWARD MORRIS.—[1688-1769]—Of Woodstock, Conn.; Lieutenant of the Woodstock Company.

REFERENCE: Savage's Genealogical Dictionary; Morris' Register; Larned's History of Windham County, Conn.

1. Seymour Morris.

LIEUTENANT JOHN MOSELEY.—[1640-1690]—Lieutenant in the Westfield Company of Foot in King Philip's War.

REFERENCE: Society of Colonial Wars Year Book, 1895, p. 256.

54. William Ward Wight.

JOHN MOSS.—(1604-1707.) Of New Haven and Wallingford, Conn. Signed the original compact on June 4, 1643. A trooper under Maj. John Mason. Representative, 1667-1673.

REFERENCES: Conn. Colonial Records, Vol. 1636-1665, p. 309; Savage's Gen. Dict., Vol. 3, p. 246.

102. Marvin Allen Ives.

JACOB MYGATT.—(1633-1706.) A member of Maj. John Mason's Troop of Horse, 1658.

REFERENCE: Bodge's Soldiers in King Philip's War, p. 467.

93. Wyllys King Smith.

LIEUTENANT SAMUEL NASH.—Of Duxbury Company prior to 1683; was private to Lieut. Wm. Holmes Company against Pequot Indians, 1637; Sheriff of Plymouth Colony, 1652; Chief Marshal of General Court, 1652; Deputy to General Court from Duxbury, 1653; Member of Council of War, 1658.

REFERENCE: Plymouth Colony Records; Savage's Dictionary.

46. George Butters.

BENJAMIN NEWBERRY.—Was a Captain in King Philip's War.

REFERENCE: Baldwin's Candee Genealogy, p. 127; Wight's The Wights, pp. 225-226; Savage's Dictionary.

54. William Ward Wight.

LIEUTENANT ANDREW NEWCOMB.—Was chosen Lieutenant at Edgartown, Mass., April 13, 1691. Was in command of the fortification there, having such number of men under him as were ordered by the Chief Magistrate.

REFERENCE: New York Colonial Records, Vol. 37, p. 230; Town Records of Edgartown, Vol. 1, p. 38.

38. George Whitfield Newcomb.
89. Albert Mattoon Graves.

EDWARD OAKES.—Arrived 1640. Selectman 29 years, between 1642 and 1678. Representative 17 years, between 1659 and 1681. Representative of Concord, 1683, 1684, and 1686. Quartermaster of the Troop in 1656. Lieutenant in Capt. Prentice's Company in King Philip's War.

REFERENCES: History of Cambridge, p. 616; Savage's Gen. Dict., p. 302.

56. Wyman Kneeland Flint.

ROGER ORVIS.—(1657-1736-7.) Soldier in King Philip's War under Capt. Newbury, and wounded at Hatfield May 16, 1676.

REFERENCE: Savage's Gen. Dict., Vol. 3, p. 317.

96. Oliver Partridge Dickinson.

RICHARD OSBORN.—Served under Lieut. Ludlow in the Pequot War. On June 4, 1639, the General Court at Hartford, Conn., granted to him for faithful service in the Pequot War 80 acres of land in Fairfield, Conn.

REFERENCES: Savage's Gen. Dict., Vol. 3, pp. 318-319.

48. Henry Austin Osborn.

JOHN OTIS.—A soldier in King Philip's War, 1675, serving in Capt. Daniel Henchman's Company, August 27, 1675. Also a member of Capt. Samuel Moseley's Company, July 24, 1675.

REFERENCES: Soldiers in King Philip's War, by Bodge, pp. 53 and 75.

78. Joseph Edward Otis, Jr.
98. Philo Adams Otis.

WILLIAM PABODIE.—(1620-1703.) Of Duxbury, Mass., and Little Compton, R. I. A member of the Duxbury Military Company under Capt. Myles Standish in August, 1643. Deputy, 1654-1663, 1670-1677, 1679-1682.

REFERENCE: Pierce's Colonial Lists, p. 75.

4. William Ruggles Tucker.

ROBERT PADDOCK.—Was a member of the Military Company at Plymouth, Mass., 1643.

REFERENCE: Pierce's Colonial Lists, p. 76.

37. Frank Bassett Tobey.

BRINTON PAINE.—[1741-1820]—Served in Capt. Saml. Chapman's Company from Bolton, Conn., in the French and Indian War.

REFERENCE: Waldo's Early History of Tolland. Conn., p. 45.

7.   Edward McKinstry Teall.

STEPHEN PAINE.—[1654-1710]—Of Rehoboth, Mass., 1675. A soldier in King Philip's War and a large contributor to the expense thereof.

REFERENCE: Paine Genealogy.

7.   Edward McKinstry Teall.

THOMAS PAINE.—Of Plymouth and Yarmouth.   Member of Yarmouth Military Company, 1643; under command of Lieut. Wm. Palmer; Deputy from Yarmouth, 1639.

REFERENCE: Pierce's Colonial Lists, p. 74; Plymouth Colonial Records.

15.   Josiah Lewis Lombard.
18.   Scott Jordan.
58.   Frederick Laforrest Merrick.

ICHABOD PALMER.—Of Stonington, Conn.   Was Ensign, Oct., 1737; Lieutenant, 1739.

REFERENCE: Connecticut Colonial Records, 1735; pp. 43, 120, 261.

10.   Edward Milton Adams.
51.   Franklin Adams Meacham.

NEHEMIAH PALMER.—Of Stonington, Conn., was Governor's Councillor, 1703. Deputy many years. Was Deputy for Stonington to Conn. General Court, 1668, and many times thereafter.

REFERENCE: Connecticut Colonial Records, 1689-1706, pp. 212.

10.   Edward Milton Adams.
51.   Franklin Adams Meacham.

ROBERT PARISH.—Of Groton and Dunstable, Mass. Was a soldier in Captain Samuel Moseley's Independent Company of Volunteers and served under Major Samuel Appleton, commanding the Mass. forces under Josiah Winslow, Commander in Chief of the Army against the Narragansetts, King Philip's War. He was a member of the garrison, Dunstable, Mass.

REFERENCE: Reprint from Pay rolls of Mr. John Hull, Treasurer at War, Mass. Bay Colony; "Soldiers in King Philip's War;" N. E. H. & G. Reg., Vol. 37, p. 182; also Vol. 43, p. 263; Mass. Archives, Vol. CVII, p. 230, Vol. LXXI, p. 83; History of Dunstable, Mass.

2.   Captain Philip Reade.

SURGEON THOMAS PARISH.—Was surgeon in Captain George Cooke's Co. in the expedition ordered on foot against Samuel Gurton in 1643.

REFERENCE: Massachusetts Colonial Records. Vol. 2, pp. 53, 346; Savage's Genealogical Dictionary, Vol. 3

2.   Captain Philip Reade.

WILLIAM PARKE.—Was member of A. & H. Artillery Co., Boston, 1638.

REFERENCE: Savage's Genealogical Dictionary; Whitman's Artillery Co., p. 148.

52.   Hobart Chatfield Chatfield-Taylor.
96.   Oliver Partridge Dickinson.

OLIVER PARTRIDGE.—(1712-1792.)   Representative to General Court at different times.   Delegate to Congress at Albany, N. Y., 1754, to confer with the Indian Six Nations.   Also delegate to first Colonial Congress in 1765.   Appointed as one of a committee, 1746-7, to direct the re-building of Fort Massachusetts.   A Colonel in the Massachusetts Bay Colonial service, 1758, and engaged in the expedition under Gen. Abercrombie for the capture of Fort Ticonderoga, 1758.

REFERENCES: Mass. Civil List; Dexter's Yale Biographies and Annals; Appleton's Encyclopaedia of American Biography; Hist. of Berkshire Co., Mass., Vol. 1, p. 83; Parkman's Montcalm and Wolfe, Vol. 2, p. 101; Winsor's Narrative and Critical Hist. of America, Vol. 5, pp. 597-598; Mass. Hist. Society Collections, 4th series, Vol. 5.

96.   Oliver Partridge Dickinson.

COL. SAMUEL PARTRIDGE.—(1645-1740.)   Quartermaster Major John Pynchon's Troop, 1688.   Deputy, 1683, '85, '86.   Associate Judge Hampshire County Court, 1685; Judge of the Court of Common Pleas, 1692-1740; member of his Majesty's Council; Colonel of Hampshire County Regiment.

REFERENCES: S. C. Wars, 1896. Year Book, p. 368; Savage's Genealogical Dictionary, Vol. 3, p. 366; Boltwood's Hadley Genealogies, p. 110; Parkman's Half Century of Conflict, Vol. 2, p. 66; American Ancestry, Vol. 5, p. 52.

96.   Oliver Partridge Dickinson.
101.   John Newbury Bagley.

JAMES PATTERSON.—(1633-1701.)   House used for Garrison during King Philip's War.

REFERENCES: Hazen's Hist. of Billerica, p. 110, 117; N. E. H. & G. R., Vol. 37, p. 148.

105.   Henry Clay Fuller.

JOSEPH PATTERSON.—(1710-1780.) Was a member of Capt. Eleazer Melvin's Company in Gov. Shirley's expedition to the Norridgewock country, 1754.

REFERENCE: N. E. Hist. and Gen. Register, Vol. 37, p. 148.

105. Henry Clay Fuller.

LIEUT. FRANCIS PEABODY.—(1614-1697.) Lieutenant in the Militia, Topsfield, Mass., 1668.

REFERENCE: S. C. W. Year Book, 1896, p. 369.
90. Edwin Fraser Gillette.

CAPT. JOHN PEABODY.—1642. Deputy to the General Court, ten terms, 1689-1730; Ensign, 1682; Lieutenant, 1691; Captain, 1699, Colony of Massachusetts Bay.

REFERENCE: S. C. W. Year Book, 1895, p. 261.
90. Edwin Fraser Gillette.

MAJOR JOHN PELL.—[1643-1702]—Second Lord of the Manor of Pelham; Member of New York Provincial Assembly for Westchester County, 1691-95; Captain of Horse, Provincial Forces, New York, 1684; Major, 1692, French and Indian War.

REFERENCE: Society of Colonial Wars Year Book, 1894; Bolton's History of Westchester; New York State Records.
12. Rodman Corse Pell.

SERGEANT JOHN PERKINS.—[1590-1654]—Was Sergeant of the Allied English and the friendly aboriginal Indians under their Chief Masconoma, at Agawam (Ipswich, Mass., Bay Colony), during the war with the Tarratines, July to September, 1631.

REFERENCE: Town Records of Ipswich; History of Ipswich; History of Essex Co., Mass., p. 200; and Gov. John Winthrop's Journal.
2. Captain Philip Reade.
96. Oliver Partridge Dickinson.

LIEUT. JACOB PERLEY.—(1670-1751.) With Capt. John Lovewell's Company, against the Indians, North Conway, N. H., 1725, and Fryburg, Maine, 1728.

REFERENCE: Military Records Mass. Archives, Vol. 72, p. 367.
90. Edwin Fraser Gillette.

ARTHUR PERRY.—Of Boston, 1630.—Member of the Ancient and Honorable Artillery Company, 1638.

REFERENCE: Savage's Genealogical Dictionary.

7. Edward McKinstry Teall.

WILLIAM PHELPS.—Was Representative to the First General Court in Mass.; Assistant in 1634; removed to Windsor, Conn., 1635; Assistant in 1636 and 1658.

REFERENCE: Savage's Gen. Dict.; Connecticut Colonial Records.

45. Francis Porter Fisher.
88. Edward Payson Bailey.

JONATHAN PHINNEY.—Ensign of Windsor, Conn.

REFERENCE: Stiles' Windsor.

72. Lester Orestes Goddard.

CORP. SOLOMON PHIPPS.—(1643——.) Charlestown. A soldier in the Mt. Hope campaign under Capt. Thomas Prentice, August 27, 1675; also under Capt. Thomas Brattle, garrison duty, December 20, 1675.

REFERENCES: Bodge's Soldiers of King Philip's War; N. E. Hist. and Gen. Register, Vol. 37, p. 280; Vol. 41, 277.

64. Harry Jenkins Bardwell.

CAPTAIN MICHAEL PIERCE.—Dec. 17, 1673, was chosen Ensign in Capt. James Endworth's Company. In 1669 commissioned Captain by the Colony Court. Was in the Great Swamp Fight, Dec. 19, 1675. After the Narragansett alarm of 1676 he was in command of the garrison of Seaconecke. Was sent to fight the hostile Indians near Pawtucket under Canonchet, having command of 50 Englishmen and 20 friendly Indians at Attleboro Gore.

REFERENCE: Pierce Genealogy.

41. John Larkin Lincoln, Jr.

SERGEANT NATHANIEL PINNEY.—Was in Captain Moses Dimond's Company of Windsor, Conn., men in the year 1711 in the expedition against Canada (Queen Anne's War, 1702-1713.)

REFERENCE: Manuscript Commissary Account of Roger Wolcott, State Archives of Connecticut; Stiles' Windsor.

72. Lester Orestes Goddard.

NATHANIEL PITKIN.—Was appointed Ensign at East Hartford May, 1716.

REFERENCE: Pitkin Genealogy; Connecticut Colonial Records, Vol. V., p. 550.

45. Francis Porter Fisher.

WILLIAM PITKIN.—Settled in Hartford about 1665; King's attorney, 1664; was Governor's Assistant, 1690 until death, 1694; Deputy, 1675-1690; Freeman, 1676; Commissioner for Connecticut to United Colonies.

REFERENCE: Pitkin Genealogy; Connecticut Colonial Records; Society of Colonial Wars Year Book, 1895.

45. Francis Porter Fisher.

CAPTAIN JONATHAN POOLE.—Of Reading, Mass. Ensign of the "Three County Troops," a Cavalry Company, in 1658. The flag of this troop was the first one designed and floated by the English Colonists in America, and Jonathan Poole was the standard bearer of this historic ensign. In King Philip's War he had a separate command of a company of foot soldiers doing duty as scouts. He was under Major Appleton at Hadley and was President of a Council of War in the winter of 1675-6.

REFERENCE: Drake, pp. 417.

57. Charles Clarence Poole.

LIEUT. JONATHAN POOLE.—In 1690 a company of troops under Capt. Savage went from Reading, Mass., on the expedition to Canada during the war with France. Jonathan Poole and Nathan Goodwin were subalterns in this company.

REFERENCES: Eaton's Gen. Hist. of Reading, p. 36.

57. Charles Clarence Poole.

THOMAS POPE.—Of Plymouth, was member of Volunteer Company from Plymouth, June 7, 1637, which, under Lieut. William Holmes and Thos. Prence, marched against Pequot Indians. He was also member of Military Co. at Plymouth in Aug., 1643.

REFERENCE: Pierce's Colonial Lists, pp. 9-84; Plymouth Colonial Records, Vol. 1, p. 61.

50. Albert Eugene Snow.

MOSES PORTER.—Enlisted in 1755 as a volunteer from the Colony of Massachusetts in the expedition planned by General Braddock against Crown Point. Captain of a Company from Hadley, Mass. In "Bloody Morning Scout," on Sept. 8, 1755, Capt. Porter was killed.

REFERENCE: "Montcalm and Wolfe," Vol. 1; History of Hadley, Mass.; Savage's Genealogical Dictionary.

45. Francis Porter Fisher.

JOSHUA PRATT.—A member of the Plymouth Military Company in August, 1643.

REFERENCE: Pierce's Colonial Lists, p. 76.

24. Lemuel Ruggles Hall.
49. Frank Eugene Spooner.

ABRAHAM PREBLE.—Was Governor's Assistant to Sir Fernando Georges at Falmouth (now Portland), Maine, 1645 to 1649; was Major of the military forces at that place under Edward Godfrey; was Assistant under Deputy Governor Henry Joselin, July 6, 1646; was authorized by Mass. to grant military commissions after 1652.

REFERENCE: New England Hist. & Gene. Register, Vol. XXII, pp. 312-15; "Preble Family in America," p. 96; Mass. Colonial Records; also N. E. Hist. & Gene. Register, Vol. 7, p. 134, quoting York Co. Records.

10. Edward Milton Adams.

GOVERNOR THOMAS PRENCE.—[1600-1678]—Governor of Plymouth Colony, 1635-1638-1658; Assistant many times. Member of Council of War and went forth against Pequot Indians in 1637; Commissioner for the United Colonies, 1645-50-61.

REFERENCE: Savage's Genealogical Dictionary, Freeman's History of Cape Cod; Plymouth Colony Records, 1635-1658.

10. Edward Milton Adams.
50. Albert Eugene Snow.
51. Franklin Adams Meacham.
58. Frederick Laforrest Merrick.
61. Victor Clifton Alderson.
90. Edwin Fraser Gillette.

SOLOMON PRENTICE.—Served as soldier in Cambridge Company in King Philip's War.

REFERENCE: Account Book of Treasurer Hall in Library of N. E. H. G. Society; Mass. Archives, Vol. 68, pp. 73, 79 and 80.

31. Charles Newton Fessenden.

JOHN PRESCOTT.—Served in garrison at Lancaster, Mass., and in defense of the town against Indians Aug. 22, 1675, and Feb. 10, 1676.

REFERENCE: Society of Colonial Wars Year Book, 1895, p. 265.

1. Seymour Morris.
14. Henry Sherman Boutell.
24. Lemuel Ruggles Hall.
81. George Henry Moore.
97. Asahel Frank Bennett.

JOHN² PRESCOTT.—Served in Garrison at Lancaster, Mass., in King Philip's War, in defense of the town against the Indians, 1675-6; also commanded a garrison at Lancaster in Queen Anne's War, 1704-5.

REFERENCE: Early Records of Lancaster, by Nourse, pp. 98, 124, 144.

    97. Asahel Frank Bennett.

JOHN³ PRESCOTT.—Served in the garrison at Lancaster, Mass., 1704-5.

REFERENCE: Nourse's Early Records of Lancaster, p. 144.

    97. Asahel Frank Bennett.

CAPTAIN JONATHAN PRESCOTT.—Of Watertown, Lancaster and Concord, Mass., was Captain of the Concord Militia in King Philip's War. His house was fortified as a garrison house in 1676.

REFERENCE: Prescott Genealogy, p. 42; N. E. H. & G. Register, Vol. 38, p. 42.

    14. Henry Sherman Boutell.
    24. Lemuel Ruggles Hall.
    81. George Henry Moore.

GENERAL ISRAEL PUTNAM.—At the outbreak of the French War, 1755, he raised a company of men in his neighborhood (Pomfret, Ct.); was appointed Captain in Lyman's Regiment; took part in the operation around Lake George and Crown Point; was promoted to rank of Major 1757. In 1758 was taken prisoner by the Indians. In 1759 became Lieut. Colonel and took an important part under Gen. Amheray in the Canadian Campaign.

REFERENCE: Connecticut Colonial Records, Vol. 1751-1757, pp. 399, 472, 539, 2, 601; Vol. 1757-1762, pp. 97, 226, 228, 356, 484, 618; Vol. 1762-1767, pp. 234, 249; Vol. 1772-1775, pp. 331, 423, 425.

    30. Chas. Durkee Dana.
    83. Alfred Henry Castle.

LIEUTENANT NATHANIEL PUTNAM.—[1619-1700]— Lieutenant of the Foot Company of Salem Village, 1683; Deputy to the Massachusetts General Court, 1690-91.

REFERENCE: Year Book, Society of Colonial Wars, 1894, pp. 122-186.

    2. Captain Philip Reade.

THOMAS PUTNAM.—Was Lieutenant of Troop of Horse in Lynn, Mass., in 1662; served in King Philip's War.

REFERENCE: Society of Colonial Wars Year Book, 1895, p. 266; Putnam Genealogy; History of Lynn.

  5. John Smith Sargent.
 30. Charles Durkee Dana.
 83. Alfred Henry Castle.
 90. Edwin Fraser Gillette.

COL. JOHN PYNCHON.—(1647-1721.) Lieutenant Colonel of Regiment.

REFERENCE: Gen. Dict., by Savage, Vol. 3, p. 498.
101. John Newbury Bagley.

MAJ. JOHN PYNCHON.—(1625-1702-3.) In command of troops in King Philip's War.

REFERENCE: Soldiers in King Philip's War, by Bodge, p. 142-145.
101. John Newbury Bagley.

WILLIAM PYNCHON.—[1590-1662]—Of Springfield, Mass. Chartered Incorporator and "Assistant" Treasurer, 1632-1634. Governor of Springfield, 1641-1650. Governing Magistrate of Connecticut, 1637-1638.

REFERENCE: Society of Colonial Wars Year Book, 1895, p. 266.
  7. Edward McKinstry Teall.

EDMUND QUINCY.—(1628-1698.) Was Magistrate of the County under the Colonial Government; was Representative in the General Court in the years 1670-73, '75-81 and '92, and possibly other years. He was one of the Military Committee of the town of Braintree; Lieutenant Colonel of the Suffolk Regiment. Appointed one of the Council of Safety for the Provisional Government; was also one of the Committee to investigate the charges against Sir Edward Andros in April, 1689. Was a Selectman of the town of Braintree for many years.

REFERENCES: Mass. Records; Hist. of Braintree; Records of Town of Quincy; Savage's Gen. Dict., Vol. 3, p. 500.
104. Charles Frederick Quincy.

JOHN RANDALL.—(——1680.) Of Watertown. A soldier in King Philip's War. Served in Capt. Poole's Company, and that of Capt. John Holbrook. Was called "Sergeant."

REFERENCES: N. E. H. & G. R., Vol. 41, p. 273, and Vol. 42, p. 99; Bodge's Soldiers in King Philip's War, pp. 260-261; Bond's Watertown, ——.
 82. Marvin Andrus Farr.

JOSHUA RAYMOND.—(1639-1676.) Of Salem, Mass., and New London, Conn. Commissary in campaign during King Philip's war, 1675. Cornet in a company of troopers raised in New London, Conn.

REFERENCES: Savage's Genealogical Dictionary. Vol. 3, p. 513, Colonial Records of Connecticut, 1665-1676, pp. 182, 186, 352, 356, 396, 266, 268, 387-390, 405.
78. Joseph Edward Otis, Jr.
98. Philo Adams Otis.

JOHN READ, SR.—(1598-1685.) Of Dorchester, Weymouth and Rehoboth. Contributed £13 18s 11d for the campaign against King Philip. A member of the Ancient and Honorable Artillery Company of Boston, 1644.

REFERENCES: Bliss' Hist. of Rehoboth, p. 117; Savage's Gen. Dict., Vol. 3, p. 516; Robert's Hist. of the A. & H. Artillery Co., Vol. 1, p. 142.
79. John Whipple Hill.

JOHN READ, JR.—(1640-1676.) Rehoboth. Killed by the Indians at Pierce's Fight, March 26, 1676.

REFERENCES: Reed's Genealogy, p. 222; Daggett's Hist. Attleborough, new edition, p. 267; Bliss History of Rehoboth, pp. 87, 91.
79. John Whipple Hill.

JOHN REED.—[1704-1771]—Lieutenant in French and Indian Wars, 1756.

REFERENCE: "Seth Read, His ancestors and descendants," by M. R. Breford, 1895, p. 16.
21. William Wolcott Strong.

JOHN REYNER.—Plymouth, Mass., 1636. Pastor Plymouth Church. Member Plymouth Military Company; Muster Roll, dated August, 1643; Will, dated Exeter, Mass., Jan. 30, 1669.

REFERENCE: Pierce's Colonial Lists, p. 76; Savage's Genealogical Dict.; "Lane Family;" "Reyner Family;" N. E. Hist. & Gen. Reg., Vol. XI. pp. 105-106.
68. Albert Judson Fisher.

HENRY RHOADES.—Fought against the Indians in the Nipmuck country; was also in "Swamp Fight," 1675.

REFERENCE: Society of Colonial Wars Year Book, 1894, p. 206.
10. Edward Milton Adams.

SAMUEL RHOADES.—Was private in Captain Ebenezer Cox's Co. from Stoughtonham, Mass., in French and Indian War, 1760. Was in Samuel Miller's Regiment at Crown Point, April to December, 1756. Was in Capt. Nathaniel Blake's Company at Crown Point, May, 1756, to March, 1757.

REFERENCE: Hunton's History Canton, Mass., pp. 641, quoting from Mass. Archives.

10. Edward Milton Adams.

EDWARD RICE.—Owned Garrison house at Marlboro, Mass. Was member of West Middlesex Regiment and quartered in his Garrison house March 18, 1691.

REFERENCE: N. E. H. & G. Reg., Vol. 43, p. 372.

17. Frederick Clifton Pierce.

SAMUEL RICE.—Was member of the garrison at the house of Joseph Rice in Marlboro, Mass., in Oct., 1675.

REFERENCE: Mass. Archives, Vol. 67, p. 277; N. E Hist. & Gen. Reg., Vol. 40, pp. 315-16.

62. William Dorrance Messinger.

THOMAS RICE.—(——1681.) Of Sudbury and Marlborough, Mass. Commanded a garrison at Marlboro in 1675. Sustained a loss of £100 at Sudbury by the Indians destroying the town in 1676.

REFERENCES: Hudson's Hist. of Marlboro', p. 68; Bodge's Soldiers in King Philip's War, p. 225.

97. Asahel Frank Bennett.

LIEUTENANT JOSIAH RICHARDSON.—[1665-1711]—Of Chelmsford, Mass. Lieutenant in West Regiment of Middlesex. Served in garrison at Chelmsford, March 16, 1691-2, during King William's War.

REFERENCE: New England Historical & Genealogical Register, Vol. 43, p. 372. Original Roll of West Regt. of Middlesex, Mass.; Memorial of the Richardson Family.

2. Captain Philip Reade.

NATHANIEL RICHARDSON.—[1651-1714]—Of Woburn, Mass.; private in Captain Prentiss' Company in the Great Swamp Fight, Dec. 19, 1675, where he was wounded.

REFERENCE: New England Historical and Genealogical Register, Vol. 37, p. 282.

1. Seymour Morris.

THOMAS ROBERTS.—Came with Hilton, 1623. Was last Colonial Governor of New Hampshire; elected April, 1640.

REFERENCE: Provincial Records of New Hampshire, Vol. 1, p. 119; Savage's Genealogical Dictionary, Vol. 3, p. 547; N. E. Hist. & Gene. Reg., Vol. 7, p. 356.

15.   Josiah Lewis Lombard.

GEORGE ROBINSON, JR.—(1656-1724.) Of Rehoboth. A soldier in King Philip's War, 1675.

REFERENCES: Baylies, Vol. 2, p. 216; Vol. 4, p. 84; Bodge's Soldiers in King Philip's War, p. 463.

82.   Marvin Andrus Farr.

JOHN ROGERS.—(——1692.) A member of Capt. Myles Standish's Company of Duxbury, Mass., in August, 1643.

REFERENCE: Pierce's Colonial Lists, p. 75.

4.   William Ruggles Tucker.

COL. ZABDIAL ROGERS.—(1737-1808.) Of Norwich, Conn. 1762, Lieutenant in the Third Regiment; 1765, Captain of the Third Regiment; 1774, Major of the Twentieth Regiment; 1777, Lieutenant Colonel; 1780, Colonel.

REFERENCE: Caulkin's Hist. of Norwich, Conn., p. 328.

71.   Ebenezer Lane.

HUGH ROWE.—(1645——.) A soldier in King Philip's War from Gloucester. His heirs received a grant of land for his services in the Indian wars.

REFERENCES: Bodge's Soldiers in King Philip's War, p. 422; Babson's Hist. of Gloucester, p. 145.

82.   Marvin Andrus Farr.

CAPT. JONATHAN RUDD.—(1738——.) Was Ensign in 1745, Lieutenant in 1750, and Captain in 1758, of the Second Company of Fifth Regiment, Connecticut Troops. Deputy, 1762 and 1764.

REFERENCES: Conn. Colonial Records, Vol. 9, pp. 164 and 555; Vol. 10, pp. 291, 326, 334; Vol. 12, pp. 73 and 241.

70.   Charles Ridgely.

JOHN RUGGLES.—Of Roxbury, Mass. Was in Captain Nicholas Manning's Company April 24, 1676. Was also in Lieutenant Gillams' Company under Major Savage. Was also Trooper under Captain Davis Jan., 1675. Was Deputy, 1658-60-61 and later.

REFERENCE: See copy of Hull's pay roll in New E. H. & G. Reg., Vol. 42, p. 95; Also Vol. 37, pp. 368-375; Massachusetts Archives, Vol. 68.

10. Edward Milton Adams.
24. Lemuel Ruggles Hall.
49. Frank Eugene Spooner.

CAPTAIN SAMUEL RUGGLES.—Of Roxbury, Mass., was Deputy four years, Captain Roxbury Militia.

REFERENCE: Mass. Colonial Records, 1654-86, p. 73.

4. William Ruggles Tucker.
24. Lemuel Ruggles Hall.

CAPT. SAMUEL RUGGLES.—(1658-1715.) Representative to the General Court of Massachusetts. Captain of the Militia.

REFERENCES: Winslow Memorial, Vol. 2, appendix, p. 25; Spooner Genealogy, pp. 246-258; History of Hardwick, Mass.; Ruggles Genealogy; Dudley Genealogy, Vol. 2, p. 903.

4. William Ruggles Tucker.
24. Lemuel Ruggles Hall.

BRIGADIER GENERAL TIMOTHY RUGGLES.—[1711-1795]—Of Rochester and Hardwick, Mass. Brigadier General and second in command at Lake George, 1755. President of Stamp Act Congress, N. Y., in 1765.

REFERENCE: Appleton's Cyclopedia of American Biography; Society of Colonial Wars Year Book.

4. William Ruggles Tucker.

WILLIAM SABIN.—(——1687.) Rehoboth. Deputy from Rehoboth, Mass., 1657, 1659, 1660, 1661, 1670, 1671. Contributed £15 5s 8d for the campaign against King Philip.

REFERENCE: Bliss History of Rehoboth, pp. 118-168.

79. John Whipple Hill.

NATHANIEL SALTONSTALL.—(——1707.) Captain of Haverhill Company, Norfolk Regiment; many years head of Essex Militia.

REFERENCES: Soldiers in King Philip's War, by Bodge. p. 475; Gen. Dict., by Savage, Vol. 4, p. 7.

101. John Newbury Bagley.

RICHARD SALTONSTALL.—[1610-1694]—Sergeant Major of Colonel Endicott's Regiment, Oct. 7, 1641. Assistant and Deputy to the General Court of Massachusetts Bay Colony, 1635-49.

REFERENCE: Society of Colonial Wars Year Book, 1895, p. 270.

54. William Ward Wight.
101. John Newbury Bagley.

HENRY SAMPSON.—[D. 1684]—Came in ship Mayflower, 1620. Private in Lieut. William Holmes' Company against Pequot Indians, 1637.

REFERENCE: Plymouth Colonial Records, Vol. 1; Giles Memorial.

46. George Butters.

ZABDIEL SAMPSON.—[1727-1776]—Private from Duxbury in French War, 1756; taken prisoner and bound to a tree, a target for Indian amusement with hatchets. Released and was killed in War of Revolution.

REFERENCE: Giles Memorial, by Vinton, p. 400; Davis' Landmarks of Plymouth, p. 229.

46. George Butters.

CAPT. JAMES SANDS.—(1622-1695.) Deputy New Shoreham County, Rhode Island, 1665; Assistant Warden, 1675. Commanded the New Shoreham Company in King Philip's War, and his house was turned into a fort and garrisoned by him.

REFERENCE: S. C. W. 1896 Year Book, p. 383; Savage's Gen. Dict. Vol. 4, p. 13; Austin's Gen. Dict. of R. I., p. 170.

78. Joseph Edward Otis.
98. Philo Adams Otis.

JOHN SARGENT.—(1639-1716.) Of Charlestown, Barnstable and Malden, Mass. A soldier under Maj. Thomas Savage in Lieut. Gillam's Company in King Philip's War.

REFERENCES: N. E. H. & G. Register, Vol. 37, p. 375; Vol. 38, p. 46; Vol. 43, p. 261; also the Sargent Genealogy.

5. John Smith Sargent.

THOMAS SAVERY.—Of Scituate; enlisted in Capt. Michael Pierce's Company; was killed by Indians in fight against Chief Canonchet, March 26, 1676.

REFERENCE: History of Plymouth Co., p. 412; Davis' Landmarks of Plymouth, p. 231.

46. George Butters.

JOSHUA SAWYER.—(1655-1738.)   Of Lancaster and Woburn, Mass., was a member of Captain Daniel Henchman's Company in King Philip's War, being credited on September 23, 1676, with £3, 7s, 0d, for services performed

REFERENCE: Bodge's Soldiers in King Philip's War, page 58.

1. Seymour Morris.

NATHANIEL SAWYER.—(1670-1756.)   Served in garrison at Lancaster, 1704-1711, and in engagements with the Indians in July and October, 1704.

REFERENCE: Nourse's Early Records of Lancaster, p. 144.

97. Asahel Frank Bennett.

PHINEAS SAWYER.—(1709-1782.)   In Capt. Eph. Wilder's Company, July, 1748; fought against Indians in "Surbody's" raid. Also "In Muster-Roll of mounted company commanded by John Carter, of Lancaster, detached out of Col. Oliver Wilder's Regiment that marched in the late alarm for Fort William Henry as far as Springfield, second Crown Point Exp., 1757."

REFERENCE: Military Annals of Lancaster, by Nourse, pp. 25 and 61.

97. Asahel Frank Bennett.

THOMAS SAWYER.—(1616-1706.)   Served in the garrison at Lancaster in King Philip's War in the defense of the town against the Indians, 1675-6.

REFERENCE: Annual Register S. C. W., p. 384.

97. Asahel Frank Bennett.

WILLIAM SAWYER.—[1603-1702]—Of Woburn, Mass. Soldier under Major Samuel Appleton of Massachusetts at the Great Swamp Fight, Dec. 19, 1675.

REFERENCE: Soldiers of King Philip's War, 1675-7, p. 108; Massachusetts Archives, Vol. 68, p. 104.

2. Captain Philip Reade.

CAPTAIN PHILIP PIETERSE SCHUYLER.—[1600-1684] —New York Provincial Forces, 1667.

REFERENCE: Society of Colonial Wars Year Book, 1894, pp. 80, 85, 101, etc.

4. William Ruggles Tucker.

CAPTAIN PAUL SEARS.—[1637-1707]—Captain in the Mass. Militia, and served in the Narragansett War.

REFERENCE: Society of Colonial Wars Year Book, 1895, p. 272.

61. Victor Clifton Alderson.
90. Edwin Fraser Gillette.

RICHARD SEARS.—Was a member of Capt. William Palmer's Company at Yarmouth, Mass., Aug., 1643; was Representative to General Court at Plymouth, 1662.

REFERENCE: Pierce's Colonial Lists, 109-74; Society of Colonial Wars Year Book, 1895.

37. Frank Bassett Tobey.
61. Victor Clifton Alderson.
90. Edwin Fraser Gillette.

MAJOR GENERAL ROBERT SEDGWICK.—[1613-1656]—Captain of Charlestown, Mass., Company, 1636; Charter Member and Captain of Ancient and Honorable Artillery Company; Commander of Castle, 1641; member of the Colonial Council of War, 1643; Major General of the Mass. forces, 1652, in the expedition against Arcadia, and also in 1656 in the expedition against Jamaica.

REFERENCE: Society of Colonial Wars Year Book, 1895, p. 273.

43. Harry Linn Wright.
109. Edwin Henry Sedgwick.

MARTIN SEVERANCE.—(1718-1810.) A soldier at Fort Dummer under Capt. Kellogg, 1738-9. Under Capt. Clessom, 1755. Under Capt. Catlin, 1756, and a member of Capt. Robert Roger's Rangers, 1758.

REFERENCES: Mass. Archives, Vol. 94, pp. 164, 421 and 555; Vol. 95, pp. 93 and 179; Sheldon's History of Deerfield, Mass., p. 157; Severance's Genealogy; Fiske's Genealogy.

84. Dr. George Foster Fiske.

CAPTAIN RICHARD SEYMOUR.—Of Hartford and Farmington, Conn.; Captain of the Seymour Fort at Kensington.

REFERENCE: Andrews' History of New Britain, Conn., p. 19; Camp's History of New Britain, Conn., p. 28.

1. Seymour Morris.

LIEUTENANT STEPHEN SEYMOUR.—Of Waterbury, Conn.; appointed Ensign of the train band in the Northbury Parish, in Waterbury, May, 1764; Lieutenant, May, 1765.

REFERENCE: Connecticut Colonial Records, pp. 253 and 349.

1. Seymour Morris.

JOHN SHATTUCK.—(——1675.) Sergeant in Capt. Richard Beer's Company, 1675. After the Squakeag fight he was drowned in crossing the Charlestown ferry.

REFERENCES: Bodge's Soldiers in King Philip's War, pp. 53 and 133; Savage's Gen. Dict., Vol. 4, p. 62.
82. Marvin Andrus Farr.

JOHN SHAW.—(——1694.) A member of the Plymouth Military Company in August, 1643.

REFERENCE: Pierce's Colonial Lists, p. 76.
4. William Ruggles Tucker.

SERGT. JOHN SHEPPARD.—Soldier in King Philip's War under Capt. Mosely. Wounded in Swamp fight.

REFERENCE: Bodge's Soldiers in King Philip's War, pp. 72 and 74.
93. Wyllys King Smith.

JOHN SHERMAN.—Of Watertown, Mass., was Ensign in 1654; Captain, 1680; Deputy, 1651-53-63.

REFERENCE: Society of Colonial Wars Year Book, 1895, p. 274.
14. Henry Sherman Boutell.
94. Henry Sherman Vail.

PHILIP SHERMAN.—(1610-1689.) First Secretary of the Providence Plantations, in 1639. Member of the Court of Commissioners, 1656. Deputy, 1665-1667.

REFERENCE: Austin's Gen. Dict. of R. I., p. 178.
78. Joseph Edward Otis, Jr.
98. Philo Adams Otis.

MOSES SIMMONS.—Of Plymouth and Duxbury, Mass. Was a member of the Duxbury Military Company in August, 1643.

REFERENCE: Pierce's Colonial Lists, p. 75.
86. John Alden Spoor.

JAMES SINCLAIR.—[1660-1731]—A soldier in King Philip's War. Was paid for service at Newbury, Mass., £2 18s. 6d. in defense of Block House.

REFERENCE: Bodge's Soldiers in King Philip's War.
39. George Samuel Marsh.

REV. SAMUEL SKELTON.—Appointed member of the Governor Endicott's Council. First Pastor of the First Church of the Puritans in America.

REFERENCE: Savage's Genealogical Dictionary; Mass. Colonial Records, Vol. 1, pp. 387, 395, 361, 57.

39. George Samuel Marsh.

JAMES SKIFF.—Was member of Lieut. John Blackmer's Co. at Sandwich, Mass., Aug., 1643.

REFERENCE: Pierce's Colonial Lists, p. 73.

4. William Ruggles Tucker.
37. Frank Bassett Tobey.

CORNELIUS BARENTSEN SLEGHT.—One of the nine original settlers of Kingston. N. Y. Sergeant of Military Company which built the Esopus stockade against the Indians by direction of Director General Peter Stuyvesant, and member of first board of Schepens, 1661. At Indian attack on Wiltwyck, June 7, 1663, Sleght was one of "the few men within the town by whom the savages, through God's mercy, were chased and put to flight," but carrying off with them over twenty women and children captives, among them a daughter of Sleght, who was forced to marry an Indian Warrior.

REFERENCE: Schoonmaker's History of New York, pp. 8, 13, 28, 30, 51 and fol. Documentary History of New York, Vol. IV, p. 29.

13. Samuel Eberly Gross.

SIMON SLOCUMB, SR.—Boston. Commander of Sloop "Seaflower," a transport in his majesty's service eastward. Served December 27, 1723, to April 24, 1724, and November 20, 1724, to September 2, 1725.

REFERENCE: Mass. Archives, Vol. 91, pp. 98 and 146.

79. John Whipple Hill.

CAPT. SIMON SLOCUMB.—(1705——.) Wrentham. Captain of a company in Col. Joseph Williams' Regiment, May 27, 1757; Captain of a company in Col. Frye's Regiment, March 31, 1759, to June 26, 1760. Served in Nova Scotia.

REFERENCES: Mass. Archives, Vol. 96, p. 112; Vol. 98, pp. 41 and 446; Vol. 79, p. 245.

79. John Whipple Hill.

SERGT. EDWARD SMITH.—(Died 1693.) Sergeant, 1662; Deputy to General Court of Rhode Island, 1665-68; "Assistant," 1691.

REFERENCE: S. C. W. Year Book, 1896, p. 389.

75. Warren Lippitt Beckwith.

HENRY SMITH.—Commissioned in March, 1636, by Massachusetts Bay Colony to govern the first settlement of Connecticut.

REFERENCES: Mass. Colonial Records, Vol. 1, p. 170; Conn. Colonial Records, Vol. 1, p. 17.
7. Edward McKinstry Teall.

JOHN SMITH.—Afterwards Reverend, was member of Lieut. Thomas Dimmock's Company at Barnstable, Mass., Aug., 1643.

REFERENCE: Pierce's Colonial Lists, p. 73.
37. Frank Bassett Tobey.

MOSES SMITH, SR.—Was Lieutenant Third Company of Lancaster Regiment, 1771-1776.

REFERENCE: Military Annals of Lancaster, by Nourse, p. 88.
97. Asabel Frank Bennett.

NEHEMIAH SMITH.—Was Ensign at New London, Conn., 1697. Was Governor's Councillor, 1703; Deputy many years.

REFERENCE: Connecticut Colonial Records, 1689-1706, p. 212.
10. Edward Milton Adams.
51. Franklin Adams Meacham.

PHILIP SMITH.—(1633-1685.) Representative from Hadley, 1677-80-84. Lieutenant of Horse.

REFERENCE: Savage, Vol. 4, p. 128.
93. Wyllys King Smith.

LIEUT. SAMUEL SMITH.—(1602-1680.) An "Ancient Serjeant" at Wethersfield, Conn., and Deputy there, 1640-1661. Lieutenant of Hadley Troop, 1663-1678, and Deputy to the General Court, Colony of Massachusetts Bay, 1661-1673; Commissioner to negotiate with the Mohawks, 1667.

REFERENCES: S. C. W., 1896 Year Book, pp. 389-390; Boltwood's Hadley Genealogies, p. 125; Savage, Vol. 4, p. 131; Sheldon, Vol. 1, p. 153.
48. Henry Austin Osborn.
64. Harry Jenkins Bardwell.
93. Wyllys King Smith.
99. Eames Mac Veagh.

MARK SNOW.—Of Eastham, Mass., was member of town "War Council" appointed Feb. 29, 1675, for Eastham; this town "War Council" had control of garrisons, etc.

REFERENCE: Pierce's Colonial Lists, pp. 97-98.
50. Albert Eugene Snow.

NICHOLAS SNOW.—1676—Of Plymouth and Eastham. Member of Plymouth Military Company, 1643; Deputy from Eastham, 1648-50 and 1662.

REFERENCE: Pierce's Plymouth Colony Civil & Mil. Lists, p. 76; Plymouth Colony Records.
15. Josiah Lewis Lombard.
18. Scott Jordan.
50. Albert Eugene Snow.
58. Frederick La Forrest Merrick.

GEORGE SOULE.—[D. 1680]—One of the signers of the compact on Mayflower, 1620; Private in Lieut. Wm. Holmes' Company against Pequot Indians, 1637; Representative to the General Court from Duxbury, 1645-46-50-51-54.

REFERENCE: Plymouth Colony Records, Vol. 1; History of Plymouth Co., p. 364.
46. George Butters.

GENERAL CONSTANT SOUTHWORTH.—[1615-1697]—Served in the Pequot War, 1637; Ensign Duxbury Company, 1646; Lieutenant, 1653; Deputy from 1647 for twenty-two years; Treasurer of Plymouth Colony sixteen years; Member of the Council of War, 1658; Commissioner for the United Colonies, 1668; Commissary General during King Philip's War; Governor of Kennebec.

REFERENCE: Society of Colonial Wars Year Book, 1895, p. 276.
15. Josiah Lewis Lombard.
63. Rev. Abbott Eliot Kittredge.

JONATHAN SPARROW.—Of Eastham, Mass. Representative, 1668, and for eighteen years after; was called Lieutenant, 1676, and Captain, 1677, in town and Colonial records; was one of town "War Council," appointed Feb. 29, 1675; was Lieutenant under Capt. John Gorham at the Swamp Fight, Dec. 19, 1675; commissioned Oct. 4, 1675; was commissioned Captain of Eastham June, 1680; was member of Colonial "War Council" in King William's War, appointed Aug. 14, 1689; was one of a commission to adjust the expenses of this war; Dec. 25, 1689.

REFERENCE: Pierce's Colonial Lists, pp. 7, 10, 68, 95, 97, 98, 104.
50. Albert Eugene Snow.
61. Victor Clifton Alderson.
90. Edwin Fraser Gillette.

RICHARD SPARROW.—A member of the Plymouth Company in August, 1643.

REFERENCE: Pierce's Colonial Lists, p. 76.

61. Victor Clifton Alderson.
90. Edwin Fraser Gillette.

ENSIGN JARED SPENCER.—[1614-1685]—Cambridge and Lynn, Mass., and Haddam, Conn. Ensign of the Raddam Military Company during King Philip's War and after; Representative to the General Court for Haddam from 1674 to 1683.

REFERENCE: Savage's Gen. Dict. of New England; Connecticut Colonial Records, Vol. II, pp. 236, 261 and 365; Vol. III, pp. 3, 17, 26, 35, 48, 115, 121; Year Book Society Colonial Wars, 1895.

68. Albert Judson Fisher.

WILLIAM SPENCER.—Of Cambridge, Mass., and Hartford, Conn. Representative from Cambridge, Mass., to General Court, 1634-1638; Lieutenant of Militia; one of the founders of the Ancient and Honorable Artillery; Deputy to the General Court of Connecticut, 1639.

REFERENCE: Savage's Gen. Dict.

72. Lester Orestes Goddard.

WILLIAM SPOONER.—A member of the Plymouth Military Company in August, 1643.

REFERENCE: Pierce's Colonial Lists, p. 76.

24. Lemuel Ruggles Hall.
49. Frank Eugene Spooner.
105. Henry Clay Fuller.

CAPTAIN JOHN SPRAGUE.—Of Charlestown, Mass. [1624-1692]—Captain of the Massachusetts forces; Deputy to the General Court, 1692.

REFERENCE: Wyman's Charlestown Genealogies; Society of Colonial Wars Year Book.

5. John Smith Sargent.

JONATHAN SPRAGUE.—Soldier in Captain Maudsley's Company.

REFERENCE: Wyman's Charlestown Genealogies; Greens Book, Malden, Mass., p. 215.

5. John Smith Sargent.

RALPH SPRAGUE.—[1637]—Representative to the General Court for nine years. Member of the A. & H. Artillery Company, 1637. Lieutenant of same, 1639.

REFERENCE: Lickford's Note Book, p. 36; Wyman's Charlestown Genealogies.

5. John Smith Sargent.

MYLES STANDISH.—[1584-1656]—February 21, 1621, he received the first military commission given in this country. In 1649 he was appointed "General in Chief" of all the companies in the Colonies.

REFERENCE: Year Book of the Society of Colonial Wars, 1894, pp. 107, 115 and 177. Records of Plymouth Colony; "Ancient Landmarks of Plymouth"; Bancroft History of the U. S., Vol. 1, p. 209; History of Duxbury, Mass.

46. George Butters.

CAPT. CHRISTOPHER STANLEY.—(1603-1646.)   Boston. A captain commanding troops in the early Indian wars of Eastern Massachusetts.

REFERENCES: Savage's Dict., Vol. 4, p. 164; Sheldon's Deerfield, Vol. 2, p. 155.

64. Harry Jenkins Bardwell.

THOMAS STANTON.—Of Hartford and Stonington, Conn. Soldier in Pequot War, 1637. Interpreter later; served in the campaign of 1637 against the Pequot Indians; was appointed Marshal, 1638; was long in charge of negotiations with Indians, being versed in their language; was Deputy from Stonington, Conn., 1666, to Connecticut legislature.

REFERENCE: Society of Colonial Wars Year Book, 1894, p. 193; Connecticut Colonial Records, 1636-78.

10. Edward Milton Adams.
51. Franklin Adams Meacham.

DR. THOMAS STARR.—(1616-1658.)   Surgeon of forces sent against the Pequots.

REFERENCE: S. C. W. 1896 Year Book, p. 393.

99. Eames Mac Veagh.

SAMUEL STEARNS, JR.—[1713-1793]—Of Amherst, Mass., and Hollis, N. H.   A private in Col. Blanchard's Regiment, 1754.   Posted on the Connecticut River, Aug. 23, 1754.

REFERENCE: N. H. State papers, Vol. 3.

39. George Samuel Marsh.

SHUABEL STEARNS.—[1655-1734]—Of Cambridge and Lynnfield, Mass.   Soldier in King Philip's War.

REFERENCE: Soldiers in King Philip's War, by Bodge.

39. George Samuel Marsh.

LIEUTENANT THOMAS STEBBINS.—Lieutenant in Captain Turner's Company at the Falls Fight in King Philip's War, May 19, 1676.

REFERENCE: Colonial Wars Year Book, 1895.
42. Charles Thomson Atkinson.

LIEUTENANT JOHN STEDMAN.—Wethersfield and Hartford, Conn. Commanded the Dragoons in the early part of King Philip's War, but died in Dec., 1675.

REFERENCE: Savage's Gene. Dictionary; Bodge's Soldiers in King Philip's War.
68. Albert Judson Fisher.

GEORGE STEELE.—(——1664.) Of Cambridge, Mass., and Hartford, Conn. One of the commissioners from Massachusetts to govern Connecticut. Representative many times from 1637-1659. Received grant of land for service performed in the Pequot War.

REFERENCES: Bodge's Soldiers in King Philip's War, p. 466; Savage's Gen. Dict., Vol. 4. p, 180.
43. Harry Linn Wright.

JAMES STEELE.—(1623-1712.) Of Hartford, Conn. Commissary for all Connecticut forces in King Philip's War. Served under Maj. John Mason in the First Connecticut Cavalry, 1658.

REFERENCES: Savage's Gen. Dict., Vol. 4, p. 180; Bodge's Soldiers in King Philip's War, p. 467.
43. Harry Linn Wright.

LIEUT. WILLIAM STICKNEY.—(1592-1665.) A founder of Rowley, Mass., in 1639. Lieutenant in 1661.

REFERENCE: S. C. W. 1896 Year Book, p. 394.
88. Edward Payson Bailey.

FRANCIS STILES.—Was commissioned Lieutenant of South Company at Woodbury, Conn., on May 10, 1773.

REFERENCE: Stiles' History of Windsor, Conn.; Connecticut, Colonial Records, 1726-35, p. 431.
52. Hobart Chatfield Chatfield-Taylor.

ANTHONY STODDARD.—Clerk of the Ancient and Honorable Artillery Company, 1642, 44, 46, 48, and was third sergeant in 1650. Deputy to the General Court twenty-three terms. Member of the Court of Commissioners, 1651-59.

REFERENCES: S. C. W. Year Book, 1896; Robert's Hist. of the Ancient and Honorable Artillery Co., pp. 96, 97.

96. Oliver Partridge Dickinson.

EBENEZER STONE.—[1670-1754]—Of Newton, Mass. Deputy to the General Court of Massachusetts, 1708-1717. Subsequently Royal Councillor of the Province of Massachusetts.

REFERENCE: Society of Colonial Wars Year Book, 1895, p. 280.

6. Lyman Dresser Hammond.

SAMUEL STONE.—Of Cambridge, Mass., and Lexington, was a member of Capt. Thomas Prentiss' Company of Troopers. He was wounded at the great Swamp Fight at Kingston, R. I., on Dec. 19, 1675. On his recovery he served again in Capt. Thos. Brattle's Troop of Horse on an expedition to Mt. Hope, in Sept., 1676.

REFERENCE: N. E. Hist. & Gen. Reg., Vol. 57, pp. 281-282; Vol. 41, p. 278.

62. William Dorrance Messinger.

REV. SAMUEL STONE.—Chaplain under Major John Mason in the Pequot War.

REFERENCE: Year Book of the Society of Colonial Wars, 1894, p. 84; Savage's Genealogical Dictionary, Vol. IV, p. 208; Connecticut Colonial Records of 1663, p. 413.

43. Harry Linn Wright.
102. Marvin Allen Ives.

SIMON STONE.—Of Groton. Served in King Philip's War, and also in King William's War. He received a grant of land in Narragansett, No. 6, for his services in the Indian War.

REFERENCES: History of Groton; Mass. Archives, Vol. 72, p. 468; Mather Magnalia; Bodge's Soldiers in King Philip's War, pp. 273, 360, 363, 436.

82. Marvin Andrus Farr.

JOHN STOW.—(——1643.) Roxbury, Mass. A member of the Ancient and Honorable Artillery in 1638. Representative to the General Court in 1639.

REFERENCES: Whitman's History of the Ancient and Honorable Artillery Co., p. 77; Savage's Gen. Dict., Vol. 4, p. 216.

77. James Harris Gilbert.

JOHN STOW.—(1641-1688.) Middletown, Conn. Soldier in the Indian Wars; wounded in the foot at Hatfield.

REFERENCES: Conn. Colonial Records of May 31, 1696; Wetmore Memorial, p. 29; Savage's Gen. Dict., Vol. 4, p. 217.
77. James Harris Gilbert.

THOMAS STOW.—(——1689.) Braintree, Mass. A member of the Ancient and Honorable Artillery Company of Boston in 1638.

REFERENCES: Whitman's History of the Ancient and Honorable Artillery Co., p. 78; Savage's Gen. Dict., Vol. 4, p. 218.
77. James Harris Gilbert.

LIEUT. THOMAS STOW.—(1674-1765.)   Middletown, Conn. Was made Ensign of the North Train Band, May, 1717. In May, 1723, he was appointed Lieutenant of the Third Militia Company of Middletown.

REFERENCES: Conn. Col. Records, Vol. 6, p. 7, and same Vol., p. 380.
78. James Harris Gilbert.

JOHN STRATTON.—Was in Major Appleton's command in Narragansett Campaign of 1675-6.

REFERENCE: Mass. Archives, Vol. 68, p. 97; N. E. Hist. & Gen. Reg., Vol. 38, p. 443.
52. Hobart Chatfield Chatfield-Taylor.

JOHN STRONG.—[1707-1793]—Was a drummer in Capt. Benj. Allyn's Company from Windsor, Conn., in the Crown Point Expedition, Aug., 1755. Ensign in Gen. Phineas Seymour's command, Siege of Montreal.

REFERENCE: Stiles' History of Windsor, Vol. 1, pp. 251, 259; Conn. War Archives, Vol. 6.
21. William Wolcott Strong.

THOMAS STRONG.—His enrollment and services in a troop of thirty-five (the first raised in the Colony of Connecticut) mustered at Windsor on March 11, 1657-8, for the protection of the Colony. This troop was commanded by Captain Richard Lord and was included in two forces under the command of Major John Mason.

REFERENCE: Records of the proceedings of the Connecticut Colonial Legislature (Trumbull's Edition) 1856, p. 309; Stiles' History of Windsor, Conn.
52. Hobart Chatfield Chatfield-Taylor.

WILLIAM SWIFT.—Was member of Lieut. John Blackmer's
Co. at Sandwich, Mass., Aug., 1643.

REFERENCE: Pierce's Colonial Lists, p. 73
37. Frank Bassett Tobey.
105. Henry Clay Fuller.

DEPUTY GOVERNOR SAMUEL SYMONDS.—[1595-1678]
—Ipswich, Mass. Deputy to the General Court, 1638-43. Assistant, 1643-73. Deputy Governor, 1673-78.

REFERENCE: Society of Colonial Wars Year Book, 1895, p. 281.
54. William Ward Wight.

ROBERT TAFT.—Was Captain of Mass. Colonial forces at
Mendon, 1735, and later; was Representative many years.

REFERENCE: Society of Colonial Wars Year Book, 1894; Annals of Mendon (Metcalf) pp. 227, 236, 238, 244, 247.
10. Edward Milton Adams.
51. Franklin Adams Meacham.

ASA TAYLOR, SR.—Of Narragansett, (now Westminster,
Mass.) was private in Capt. Asa Whitcomb's Co. of Colonel Bagley's Regiment, raised about 1757 for the reduction of
Canada; was in service March to December, 1758; was again
recruited 1759.

REFERENCE: Heywood's History of Westminster. p. 102.
52. Hobart Chatfield Chatfield-Taylor.

SURGEON OLIVER TEALL.—Was born in New Haven,
Conn., studied medicine and surgery, removed to Killingworth,
Conn., entered the English Army as a Surgeon, and served
through the French War.

REFERENCE: Genealogical and Historical Notes of the Teall
Family.
7. Edward McKinstry Teall.

MAJOR EPHRAIM TERRY.—(1701-1795.) Enfield, Conn.
Justice Hartford County; Captain of Train Band, 1751; Major
of Train Band.

REFERENCES: Conn. Colonial Records, Vol. 10, p. 53; Notes
of Terry Families, by Stephen Terry, A. M., Hartford, Conn., 1887,
p. 10.
21. William Wolcott Strong.
40. Chandler Pease Chapman.

STEPHEN TERRY.—[1668]—Of Windsor, Conn., was a member of Capt. Lord's Company of "Troopers," the first body of horse raised in New England; was mustered in March 11, 1657.

REFERENCE: Savage's Genealogical Dictionary; Connecticut Colonial Records, Vol. 1636-1665, p. 309; S. C. W. Year Book, 1895, p. 283.

10. Edward Milton Adams.
43. Harry Linn Wright.
52. Hobart Chatfield Chatfield-Taylor.

NATHANIEL THOMAS, SR.—(1606-1675.) Marshfield, Mass., 1643; was a Lieutenant and Captain of Marshfield Company.

REFERENCES: Savage's Gen. Dict., Vol. 4, p. 281; Bodge's Soldiers in King Philip's War, pp. 455-457.

78. Joseph Edward Otis, Jr.
98. Philo Adams Otis.

NATHANIEL THOMAS.—(1643-1718.) Marshfield, Mass. Representative 1672 and served years thereafter. A Captain in King Philip's War and a member of the Governor's Council.

REFERENCES: Savage's Gen. Dict., Vol. 4, pp. 481 and 482.

78. Joseph Edward Otis, Jr.
98. Philo Adams Otis.

WILLIAM THOMAS.—(1573-1651.) Marshfield, Mass. Assistant in 1642, 1643, 1644, 1647, 1651.

REFERENCE: Savage's Gen. Dict., Vol. 4, p. 282.

78. Joseph Edward Otis, Jr.
98. Philo Adams Otis.

CAPTAIN SAMUEL THOMPSON.—Lieutenant, and later Captain of first Company New Haven Train Band; Deputy to General Assembly, 1716.

REFERENCE: Colonial Records of Connecticut, 1705-1716, p. 143, 394, 546.

42. Charles Thomson Atkinson.

JOHN THURSTON.—Of Dedham, Mass. Served against the Indians 1675-6.

REFERENCE: N. E. Historical & Gen. Register, Vol. 43, p. 272.

  5. John Smith Sargent.
 10. Edward Milton Adams.
 40. Frank Eugene Spooner.
 51. Franklin Adams Meacham.

LIEUTENANT THOMAS THURSTON.—In 1675 was a Sergeant, promoted to Lieutenant in 1678, doing good service in King Philip's War. In 1676 he represented Medfield, Mass., in the General Court of Mass.

REFERENCE: Thurston Family Genealogy; History of Medfield.

 70. Charles Ridgely.

JOHN TILLEY.—(——1621.) Signer of the Compact on the "Mayflower," 1620. In the first encounter at Great Meadow Creek, December 6, 1620.

REFERENCE: Foot note to p. 83, Bradford's History, Plymouth Plantation.

  4. William Ruggles Tucker.
  5. John Smith Sargent.
 93. Wyllys King Smith.
105. Henry Clay Fuller.

THOMAS TOBEY, SR.—Was a member of Council of War for town of Sandwich, Mass. Appointed Feb. 29, 1676. [He was granted fifty to sixty acres of land July 7, 1681, for services in King Philip's War.] At a Council of War held at Marshfield, Feb. 29, 1676, Thomas Tobey, Sr., was appointed one of council for town and other military forces at that town, could enroll and impress men, etc.

REFERENCE: Freeman's History of Cape Cod, Vol. 1, p. 255; Vol. 1, p. 295; Plymouth Colony Records, Vol. 6, pp. 66; Vol. V, p. 196.

 37. Frank Bassett Tobey.

CAPTAIN THOMAS TOPPING.—Captain of the Southampton, L. I., Militia, 1651; Assistant, 1655-8, 1659-63.

REFERENCE: Savage's Genealogical Dictionary, Vol. 4, pp. 255; Howell's History East Hampton, p. 32; Palfrey's New England, Vol. 2, p. 638.

 25. Frank Baker.
 51. Franklin Adams Meacham.

JOHN TOWER.—(1609-1702.) Of Tower's Garrison House during King Philip's War.

REFERENCES: R. I. Colonial Records; S. C. W. 1896 Year Book, p. 401.

79. John Whipple Hill.
82. Marvin Andrus Farr.

LIEUTENANT JOHN TRACY.—Was Ensign of the Military Company at Duxbury, Mass., 1682; was appointed Lieutenant Oct. 2, 1689. Plymouth Colonial forces. Was Deputy to the General Court from Norwich, 1683-86.

REFERENCE: Pierce's Colonial Lists; Plymouth Colony Records, Vol. V, pp. 84 and 218.

10. Edward Milton Adams.
51. Franklin Adams Meacham.

SOLOMON TRACY.—Commissioned Ensign in 1698; Lieutenant, 1701; Deputy to General Court twelve sessions; in 1711 Clerk of the House; in 1717 Speaker of the House.

REFERENCE: Conn. Colonial Records, Vol. 3.

70. Charles Ridgely.

LIEUTENANT THOMAS TRACY.—[1610-1685]—Ensign First Train Band, Norwich, Conn., 1666; in 1672 Lieutenant of New London Co. Dragoons, enlisted to fight the Dutch and Indians. Member of the General Court twenty-seven sessions. Commissary in King Philip's War.

REFERENCE: Society of Colonial Wars Year Book, 1895, p. 285.

64. Harry Jenkins Bardwell.
70. Charles Ridgely.
71. Ebenezer Lane.

CORPORAL RICHARD TREAT.—(1622-1693.) Corporal in Wethersfield Troop of Horse, 1658. The first troop in the Colony of Connecticut.

REFERENCES: S. C. W. Register 1895, p. 256; Treat Genealogy, p. 35.

93. Wyllys King Smith.

RICHARD TREAT.—[1590-1669]—Of Wethersfield, Conn., 1669; Representative to the General Court and re-elected many times; Assistant Magistrate of the Colony, 1658-1665; named in the Royal Charter of Charles II. as one of the patentees for Connecticut, 1662.

REFERENCE: Society of Colonial Wars Year Book, 1894, p. 55; Year Book, 1895, p. 266.

 1. Seymour Morris.
15. Josiah Lewis Lombard.
33. Deming Haven Preston.
43. Harry Linn Wright.
63. Rev. Abbott Eliot Kittredge.
93. Wyllys King Smith.

GOVERNOR ROBERT TREAT.—[1622-1710]—Commander at Great Swamp Fight; Major commanding Connecticut Troops at the Battles of Hadley and Springfield; Deputy Governor, 1676-86; appointed Governor, 1686; resigned, 1701; in the encounter with the Indians at Bloody Brook, Sept. 18, 1675, his arrival on the scene of action with the Connecticut forces turned the tide.

REFERENCE: Society of Colonial Wars Year Book, 1895, p. 266.

15. Josiah Lewis Lombard.
63. Rev. Abbott Eliot Kittredge.

LIEUTENANT JAMES TROWBRIDGE.—[1636-1717]—Of Newton, Mass. Deputy to the General Court from Cambridge, 1700-1703. Served in King Philip's War.

REFERENCE: Society of Colonial Wars Year Book, 1895, p. 296.

 6. Lyman Dresser Hammond.

CAPTAIN MOSES TUCKER.—Of New Ipswich, N. H. His house was fortified and used as a garrison for the neighborhood during the Indian raid on the town. He was a Captain in the French and Indian War.

REFERENCE: N. H. Archives; History of Ipswich, N. H., p. 437.

 4. William Ruggles Tucker.

NATHANIEL TURNER.—Captain, ——, 1647. Captain in Pequot War; Assistant, 1639.

REFERENCE: Savage's Gen. Dictionary.

43. Harry Linn Wright.

SAMUEL UFFORD.—Was appointed Ensign of Stratford, Conn., May 13, 1714; promoted Lieutenant May 12, 1720.

REFERENCE: Connecticut Colonial Records, 1706-1716, p. 429; Vol. 1717-1725, p. 175.

59. Charles Pratt Whitney.

LIEUTENANT PHINEAS UPHAM.—Entered service about September, 1675, under Captain Isaac Johnson, and took part with his company, Dec. 19, 1675, in the storming of Fort Cononicus, or the battle of the Great Swamp Fort. Capt. Johnson being killed in this battle, Lieut. Upham succeeded him in command and was himself severely wounded.

REFERENCE: Military Records, Vol. 1, 280; also page 276; Mass. Archives, Vol. 68, p. 104; Year Book Society of Colonial Wars, 1894, pp. 31 and 208.

29. Frederic William Upham.
55. Gov. William Henry Upham.

HEZEKIAH USHER, SR.—(——1676.) Boston and Billerica, Mass. A member of the Ancient and Honorable Artillery Company of Boston, in 1638. Ensign of that Company in 1664. Representative to the General Court for Billerica, in 1671-3.

REFERENCES: Whitman's History of the Ancient and Honorable Artillery Co., p. 74; Savage's Gen. Dict., Vol. 4.

77. James Harris Gilbert.

OLOFF STEVENSON VAN CORTLANDT.—[1600-1684]— In 1649, Colonel of the "City Train Band," and in 1655-1664, the last Burgomaster of New Amsterdam, under the Dutch, before the English conquest.

REFERENCE: Society of Colonial Wars Year Book, 1894, pp. 29, 34, 55, etc.

4. William Ruggles Tucker.

COLONEL STEPHANES VAN CORTLANDT.—[1643-1710] —Kings County Regiment, 1671-1693; Mayor of New York City, 1677; Member of King's Council, 1680-1700.

REFERENCE: Society of Colonial Wars Year Book, 1894, pp. 45, 91, 97, etc.

4. William Ruggles Tucker.

BRANT ARENT VAN SCHLICHTENHORST—First resident director of the Colony of Rensselaerwick, 1646-8, and Commander of the Fort at Rensselaerwick.

REFERENCES: S. C. W. Year Book, p. 406; Mag. of Amer. Hist., Vol. 11, pp. 1 to 32.

4. William Ruggles Tucker.

LIEUTENANT GOVERNOR GEORGE VAUGHAN.—[1676-1725]—Colonel of Provincial Forces during Queen Anne's War; elected by General Assembly, 1707; Representative of Province to England; appointed Lieutenant Governor of the Province, commission dated July 18, 1715; resigned Sept. 30, 1717.

REFERENCE: History of Cutt family, p. 503.

46. George Butters.

WILLIAM VAUGHAN.—[1640-1719]—In 1672 was Lieutenant of Cavalry under Captain Robert Pike; Captain in 1680; in 1681 was promoted to Major, commanding the Militia of the Province.

REFERENCE: History of Cutt family, p. 489; Savage's Genealogical Dictionary, Adjutant Gen. Reports of N. H.

46. George Butters.

JONATHAN WADE.—Called Major and Captain. Captain of the Three County Troops of Horse.

REFERENCE: Savage's Genealogical Dictionary, p. 378; History of Medford, Mass.; N. E. Hist. & Gen. Register, Vol. XLIII, p. 274; Soldiers in King Philip's War.

5. John Smith Sargent.
57. Charles Clarence Poole.

CAPTAIN JOHN WADSWORTH.—Was a Lieutenant and Captain in King Philip's War. A Representative in the General Assembly from Hartford. On Oct. 31, 1687, he secreted the charter of Connecticut, granted by Charles II. in 1662, in an oak tree in Hartford, on Wyllys Hill, to prevent the same being taken by Sir Edmund Andros, who came to Hartford with sixty men to wrest it by force from the Colonists.

REFERENCE: Trumbull's History Connecticut, Vol. 1, p. 391; Savage's Genealogical Dictionary, Vol. 4, p. 380; Wadsworth Family in America, p. 85; Year Book, 1894, Society of Colonial Wars, p. 197.

43. Harry Linn Wright.

BENJAMIN WAIT.—Of Hatfield, Mass., was Sergeant; killed by Indians at Deerfield, Mass., Feb. 29, 1704.

REFERENCE: Savage's Gen. Dict.; Judd's History of Hadley, Mass.

60. John Conant Long.
96. Oliver Partridge Dickinson.

JOSEPH WAIT.—Enlisted May, 1754, in Captain Eleazer Melvin's Company. In December, 1754, Corporal in John Burk's Company of Rangers, and was stationed at Falltown. He served in the expedition to Crown Point and in Colonel Ephraim William's Regiment in the Battle of Lake George, Sept. 8, 1755, and became an Ensign in this Regiment when commanded by Seth Pomeroy, after the death of Colonel Williams. In the winter of 1756 he served at Fort Edward and Fort William Henry when the Regiment was commanded by Colonel Joseph Dwight; was transferred to Major Robert Roger's corps of Rangers in January, 1757; participated in the fight at "Roger's Slide," Lake George.

REFERENCE: Published Journal of Major Robert Rogers; Society of Colonial Wars Year Book. 1895, p. 11.

26. Horatio Loomis Wait.

CAPT. JOHN WAITE.—(1618-1693.) Lieutenant of Malden, Mass. Colonial Forces, 1658. Captain, 1662-1684. Led detachment of soldiers to Marlborough, 1675. Served in King Philip's War under Maj. John Pynchon. Deputy to General Court eighteen years. Speaker of the House of Deputies, in 1684.

REFERENCES: S. C. W. 1896 Year Book, p. 412; N. E. H. & G. Register, Vol. 32, p. 189.

99. Eames Mac Veagh.

MAJOR RICHARD WALDRON.—[1616-1689]—Representative to the General Court, 1651-57-61; was one of Council under new form of government of New Hampshire, 1680; on death of President Cutt, 1681, was head of the Province until arrival of Royal Governor. He was Captain in early days and Major in the Indian War, 1675-6. He was killed by the Indians.

REFERENCE: Savage's Dictionary; Adjutant Gen. Reports, N. H.

46. George Butters.

EBENEZER WALKER.—(1716-1799.)   Rehoboth, Mass. Private in Captain Jonathan Peck's Company, 1746.

REFERENCE: See Mass Archives, Vol. 92, p. 43.

79. John Whipple Hill.

PHILLIP WALKER.—(——1679.)   Rehoboth.   Deputy from Rehoboth, Mass., 1669. Contributed £26 for the campaign against King Philip.

REFERENCES: Walker Genealogy. p. 119;   Bliss' History Rehoboth, pp. 118-168; Mass. Archives, Vol. 68, p. 154; Year Book S. C. W., 1896, pp. 153-219.

79. John Whipple Hill.

JOHN WARD.—His house was built by him for and used as a garrison during King Philip's War, 1675.

REFERENCE: Society of Colonial Wars Year Book, 1895, p. 292.
31. Charles Newton Fessenden.

WILLIAM WARD.—In garrison at Sudbury, Mass., in King Philip's War.

REFERENCE: Society of Colonial Wars Year Book, 1895, p. 292.
31. Charles Newton Fessenden.

CAPTAIN JOSEPH WARNER.—Of Hardwick, Mass. Captain in the French War. Commanded a Company that marched for the relief of Fort William Henry, August 9, 1757.

REFERENCE: History of Hardwick.
72. Lester Orestes Goddard.

NATHANIEL WARNER.—(1656-1714.) Of Hadley, Mass. Served as private, King Philip's War.

REFERENCES: Soldiers of King Philip's War, by George M. Bodge, p. 151; Savage's Gen. Dict., Vol. 4, p. 421.
105. Henry Clay Fuller.

DANIEL WARREN.—Of Watertown, Mass. A soldier in King Philip's War.

REFERENCE: Society of Colonial Wars Year Book, 1895, p. 293; N. E. Hist. & Gen. Register, Vol. 43, p. 279.
4. William Ruggles Tucker.
67. John Demmon Vandercook.

JAMES WARRINER.—[1641-1727]—Springfield, Mass., Aug. 19, 1668, he was sent as a soldier by Col. Pynchon to the relief of Quabang (Brookfield). He was again sent by Col. Pynchon on Sept. 21, 1688, under command of Henry Gilbert, to scout for Indians about Brookfield and to make fortifications there. They built the Gilbert Fort, which served Brookfield in future wars.

REFERENCE: Savage's Genealogical Dict.; History of Springfield, by M. A. Greene, pp. 194-262; "West Springfield Centennial," p. 97; History of North Brookfield, pp. 140, 141 and 153.
68. Albert Judson Fisher.

JOHN WASHBURN.—Of Duxbury, Mass., 1645 was in an expedition fitted out that year against the Narragansetts and their confederates; and the town of Duxbury furnished six men "wch went wth those that went first," and "were forth XVII dayes."

REFERENCE: Winsor's History of Duxbury, Mass.; Plymouth Colony Records, Vol. II, p. 90.

34. Hempstead Washburne.
90. Edwin Fraser Gillette.

JOHN WASHBURN, JR. A member of the Duxbury Military Company, in August, 1643.

REFERENCE: Pierce's Colonial Lists, p. 75.

90. Edwin Fraser Gillette.

DAVID WATERBURY.—Was appointed Ensign of Fairchild Co. Dragoons, April, 1690; was appointed Lieutenant of Stamford Train Band 1698; he served in King Philip's War, 1675-6.

REFERENCE: Connecticut Colonial Records, Vol. 10, pp. 21, 253; Huntington's History of Stamford, pp. 113-14.

10. Edward Milton Adams.

ENSIGN THOMAS WATERMAN.—(1644-1708.) Sergeant of Militia, Ensign of Dragoons for New London County, 1690; Ensign of Norwich Train Band, 1708.

REFERENCES: Caulkin's History of Norwich, p. 206; Conn. Colonial Records, Vol. 1689-1706, p. 21; Vol. 1606-1616, p. 68; 1896 Year Book, p. 411.

64. Harry Jenkins Bardwell.

LAWRENCE WATERS.—[1687]—A soldier in the garrison at Lancaster, 1675, and earlier. One of the three first settlers of Lancaster, Mass. Soldiers in King Philip's War, East side of North River.

REFERENCE: Society Colonial Wars Year Book, 1895, p. 293; Marvin's "History of Lancaster," pp. 61 and 110; Nourse's "Early Records of Lancaster," pp. 128, 133, 139.

4. William Ruggles Tucker.
18. Scott Jordan.
26. Horatio Loomis Wait.
67. John Demmon Vandercook.
68. Albert Judson Fisher.

GEORGE WATSON.—(1603-1689.) Of Plymouth, Mass. A member of the Plymouth Military Company in August, 1643.

REFERENCE: Pierce's Colonial Lists, p. 76.
4. William Ruggles Tucker.

GOVERNOR JOHN WEBSTER.—[——1661]—Hartford, 1636; Representative, 1637; Magistrate, 1639 to 1655; Deputy Gov. of Connecticut, 1655; Governor of Connecticut, 1656; one of the commissioners of the United Colonies.

REFERENCE: Savage's Dictionary; Society of Colonial Wars Year Book, 1895, p. 293.
43. Harry Linn Wright.
64. Harry Jenkins Bardwell.
93. Wyllys King Smith.

ROBERT WEBSTER.—[——1676]—Lieutenant, 1654; in service in war of 1675.

REFERENCE: Savage's Genealogical Dictionary.
43. Harry Linn Wright.
93. Wyllys King Smith.

ALEXANDER WELLS.—(1727-1813.) Of Washington County, Pa. He built and maintained a stockade fort on Cross Creek during the Indian War, known as "Lord Dunmore's War."

REFERENCES: Crumrime's History of Washington Co., Pa., pp. 73, 721, 722 and 736; Washington and Irving Correspondence, by Butterfield, pp. 291 to 300.
95. William John Moore.

GOVERNOR THOMAS WELLS.—[1598-1660]—Of Wethersfield, Conn.; Magistrate of Governing Court, 1637-60; Second Treasurer, 1639-51; Secretary, 1640-48; Governor (pro tem.) 1651; Deputy Governor, 1654-56-57-59; Governor, 1655-58; Commissioner for United Colonies, 1649.

REFERENCE: Society of Colonial Wars Year Book, 1895, p. 294.
69. Samuel Rogers Wells.
96. Oliver Partridge Dickinson.
100. Nelson Cowles Gridley.

WILLIAM WESTWOOD.—[1606-1669]—One of the commissioners appointed by Mass. Bay Colony to govern the Colony of Connecticut, 1636; Assistant Connecticut Colony, 1637.

REFERENCE: Society Colonial Wars Year Book, 1895, p. 295.
43. Harry Linn Wright.
45. Francis Porter Fisher.
64. Harry Jenkins Bardwell.

CHRISTOPHER WHEATON.—Soldier in King Philip's War, under Capt. Isaac Johnson and Captain John Jacob, March 24, 1675.

REFERENCE: N. E. Hist. & Gen. Register, Vol. XXXIX, pp. 76-78; History of Hingham, 1894-5; Converse Genealogy, 1892-3.

5. John Smith Sargent.

JOHN WHEELER.—Of Concord, 1642; served in Captain Davenport's Company in Great Swamp Fight.

REFERENCE: New England Historical and Genealogical Register, Vol. 39, pp. 258 and 261.

25. Frank Baker.

LIEUTENANT JOSEPH WHEELER.—Lieutenant of the Concord Militia in King Philip's War.

REFERENCE: New England Historical and Genealogical Register, Vol. 43, p. 276.

24. Lemuel Ruggles Hall.

SERGEANT THOMAS WHEELER.—[1628-1704]—Sergeant in Captain Timothy Wheeler's Company of Concord, Mass., and under Major Willard.

REFERENCE: Shattuck's Concord, p. 46; New England Historical and Genealogical Register, Vol. 37, p. 84; Vol. 38, p. 224.

25. Frank Baker.

CAPTAIN TIMOTHY WHEELER.—[1697-1782]—A member of Concord, Mass., Militia.

REFERENCE: Concord Records p. 432.

26. Frank Baker.

TIMOTHY WHEELER.—Captain from Concord, Mass.; served in King Philip's War; Deputy nine years from 1663.

REFERENCE: Society of Colonial Wars Year Book, 1895, p. 295.

14. Henry Sherman Boutell.
81. George Henry Moore.

CAPTAIN DAVID WHIPPLE.—(1714-1766.) Cumberland, R. I. Representative to General Assembly Colony of R. I., 1756 and 1757.

REFERENCES: R. I. Colonial Records, Vol. 6, p. 487; Vol. 6, p. 3.

79. John Whipple Hill.

ENSIGN JEREMIAH WHIPPLE.—(1663-1721.) Rehoboth.
Ensign in 6th Co. (Capt. Jerard Talbot), Second Regiment
(Col. Winthrop Hilton), in the expedition against Nova Scotia.
Commission dated April 23d, 1707.

REFERENCES: Mass. Archives, Vol. 71, p. 300; Rehoboth Rec.,
1715-1805, p. 34.

   79.   John Whipple Hill.

CAPTAIN JOHN WHIPPLE.—(1617-1685.) Providence, R.
I. In 1666, 1669, 1675, 1676 Deputy to General Assembly of
R. I. 1676 he helped defend Providence during the attack of
the Indians, and he is mentioned as with others in search of
the enemy; 1679 he was appointed by the General Assembly
of Rhode Island as one of a committee to give an account of
the late war with the Indians and make returns to this Assembly.

REFERENCES: Drake's Hist. of Boston, Folio 417; Annals of
the Town of Providence, Staples; History of Providence County,
1891; R. I. Historical Tracts; R. I. Colonial Records, Vol. 2, 1664-77,
p. 150; Gen. Dict. of R. I., Austin, p. 221.

   75.   Warren Lippitt Beckwith.
   79.   John Whipple Hill.
   82.   Marvin Andrus Farr.

CAPTAIN JOHN WHIPPLE.—[1626-1683]—Lieutenant in
Capt. John Appleton's Troop, 1668. Lieutenant of Capt. Nicho-
las Paige's Company in the first, or Mount Hope Campaign.
King Philip's War, 1675. Captain of Spanish Troop in 1676.
Deputy to General Court, 1674-79-82-83.

REFERENCE: Society of Colonial Wars Year Book, 1895, p. 295.

   14.   Henry Sherman Boutell.
   24.   Lemuel Ruggles Hall.
   73.   Anthony French Merrill.

COLONEL JOSEPH WHIPPLE.—(1662-1746.) Providence.
Deputy to General Court of Rhode Island, 1698-1728. Assistant,
1714, Colonel of Land Forces, 1719-20.

REFERENCE: S. C. W. Year Book, 1896, p. 415.

   75.   Warren Lippitt Beckwith.

JOHN WHITCOMB.—Of Dorchester, Scituate and Lancaster,
Mass. In August, 1643, a member of Military Company of Scituate.

REFERENCE: Pierce's Colonial Lists, p. 74

   4.   William Ruggles Tucker.
  26.   Horatio Loomis Wait.
  67.   John Demmon Vandercook.

JOSIAH WHITCOMB.—(1638-1718.) Was a member of the garrison at Lancaster on April 20, 1704.

REFERENCES· N. E. H. & G. R., Vol. 43, p. 371; Hist. Lancaster, p. 133.

4. William Ruggles Tucker.
67. John Demmon Vandercook.

CAPTAIN DANIEL WHITE.—(1671-1726.) Ensign, 1711, in Queen Anne's War. Captain of Troop, 1716, Colony of Connecticut.

REFERENCE: S. C. W. Year Book, 1896.

96. Oliver Partridge Dickinson.

LIEUT. DANIEL WHITE.—(——1713.) Lieutenant of Hatfield, Mass. Company, 1692.

REFERENCE: S. C. W. Year Book, 1896.

96. Oliver Partridge Dickinson.

CAPTAIN JOEL WHITE.—(1705-1789.) Represented Bolton, Conn., in legislature at 26 sessions between 1750 and 1773. Lieutenant of Company or Train Band in Bolton, Conn., in 1746; Captain, 1755.

REFERENCES: Conn. Colonial Records, Vol. 9, p. 40; Vol. 10, p. 355; Kellogg's Memorial, Elder John White.

96. Oliver Partridge Dickinson.

LIEUT. JOHN WHITE.—(1642-1695.) Of Roxbury and Brookline, Mass. Lieutenant of the Militia.

REFERENCES: Savage's Gen. Dict., Vol. 4, p. 511; The Bowens of Woodstock, p. 174.

30. Charles Durkee Dana.
83. Alfred Henry Castle.

SERGT. JOSIAH WHITE. Commanded a garrison on "Ye West Side Penecook River, called Ye Neck," at Lancaster, 1704-1711, and fought against the Indians, July and October, 1704.

REFERENCE: Early Records of Lancaster, by Nourse, p. 111.

97. Asahel Frank Bennett.

REV. JOHN WHITING.—[—— 1689]—Was Chaplain of Hartford forces in King Philip's War.

REFERENCE: Society of Colonial Wars Year Book, 1895.

45. Francis Porter Fisher.

WILLIAM WHITING.—[—— 1647]—Elected to Court of Magistrates, 1637; Treasurer of Connecticut Colony, 1641-1647; chosen Major, 1642.

REFERENCE: Colonial Records of Connecticut, Vol. 1, p. 496; Trumbull's History of Hartford Co., Vol. 1, p. 269; Savage's Gen. Dict., Vol. 4, p. 521.

21. William Wolcott Strong.
40. Chandler Pease Chapman.
93. Wyllys King Smith.

FRANCIS WHITMORE.—[1625-1685]—Of Cambridge. Served in Indian wars under Major Simon Willard.

REFERENCE: Society of Colonial Wars Year Book, 1895, p. 296.
18. Scott Jordan.
62. William Dorrance Messinger.

ENSIGN THOMAS WHITMORE.—[1673-1752]—Of Cambridge, Mass., and Killingly, Conn. May, 1742, commissioned Ensign of the Third Company or Train Band of Killingly. Deputy from Killingly to General Assembly, 1720-25 and 1729.

REFERENCE: Connecticut Colonial Records, Vol. 8, p. 449.
18. Scott Jordan.

JOHN WHITNEY.—[1624-1692]—A member of Capt. Hugh Mason's Company of Watertown, Mass. Enrolled in 1675. Served in the Sudbury fight, April 29, 1676.

REFERENCE: Massachusetts Archives, Vol. 68, p. 74; Forbush Genealogy; Bond's History of Watertown; Society of Colonial Wars Year Book, 1895, p. 296; Pierce's Whitney Genealogy, pp. 23 and 24.

17. Frederick Clifton Pierce.
18. Scott Jordan.
26. Horatio Loomis Wait.
45. Francis Porter Fisher.
49. Frank Eugene Spooner.
59. Charles Pratt Whitney.
82. Marvin Andrus Farr.

MOSES WHITNEY.—(1655——.) Of Concord, Sudbury and Stow, Mass. A soldier in King Philip's War.

REFERENCES: Whitney Genealogy, p. 493; S. C. W., 1896 Year Book, p. 416.
87. Dr. Eugene Wolcott Whitney.

JOHN WICKES.—(1609-1675.) One of the Commissioners to treat with the Narragansett Indians. Deputy, 1664-73, and 1675. Assistant, 1650-55. Killed by the Indians in King Philip's War, March 17th, 1675.

REFERENCE: S. C. W. Year Book, 1896, p. 417.
75. Warren Lippitt Beckwith.

SERGEANT SAMUEL WILBOUR.—Of Portsmouth, R. I. Chosen Clerk of the Train Band, June 27, 1638; appointed Sergeant, 1644.

REFERENCE: Austin's Genealogical Dictionary of R. I.

4. William Ruggles Tucker.

GEORGE WILLARD.—A member of the "Scituate Company" of Plymouth Colony; active service, 1643-4.

REFERENCE: Society of Colonial Wars Year Book, 1895, p. 297.

61. Victor Clifton Alderson.
90. Edwin Fraser Gillette.

MAJOR SIMON WILLARD.—[1605-1676]—Founder of Concord, Mass., 1630. He was Deputy, 1630 to 1649. Assistant, 1651 and held that office until the time of his death. Commissioned Lieutenant Commandant March, 1637, in the Train Band; promoted Captain of the Colonial forces, 1646, and again Sergeant Major in command of the Middlesex regiment in 1653, and held same for 23 years. Was Commander in Chief against the Niantics in 1654. Commanded the Middlesex regiment of Massachusetts Troops in King Philip's War. Led the relief at the battle of Brookfield, August, 1675. Fought, defeated and dispersed the Indians who had attacked Groton, March 17, 1676.

REFERENCE: History of Concord, Mass.; History of Chelmsford, Mass.; Colonial Records of Massachusetts, pp. 122, 152, 180, 181, 187, 194, 210 and 214; Year Book, General Society of Colonial Wars.

2. Captain Philip Reade.
26. Horatio Loomis Wait.

SERGEANT CHARLES WILLIAMS.—Born, 1691. Sergeant in Haddam, Conn., Company in the Indian Wars.

REFERENCE: East Haddam Records.

56. Wyman Kneeland Flint.

ISAAC WILLIAMS.—Was commissioned Lieutenant at Cambridge May 26, 1647.

REFERENCE: Mass. Col. Records, Vol. 5, p. 173

52. Hobart Chatfield Chatfield-Taylor.

ROBERT WILLIAMS.—(1608-1693.) Roxbury, Mass. A member of the Ancient and Honorable Artillery Company of Boston, 1644.

REFERENCES: 1896 Year Book, p. 418; Hist. A. & H. Artillery, pp. 136, 146 and 147.

64. Harry Jenkins Bardwell.
96. Oliver Partridge Dickinson.

GOVERNOR ROGER WILLIAMS.—(1599-1683.) Captain of Train Band at Providence during King Philip's War. Governor of Rhode Island, 1654.

REFERENCE: S. C. W. Year Book, 1896, p. 418.
75. Warren Lippitt Beckwith.

CAPTAIN STEPHEN WILLIAMS.—(1640-1720.) Roxbury, Mass. Captain of Troop of Horse in command of frontier, 1707-1712. In 1710 his troop served as guard to Colonel Schuyler and the Maqua Indians.

REFERENCES: 1896 Year Book, p. 418; Wyman's Charlestown, p. 1034.
64. Harry Jenkins Bardwell.

DEPUTY-GOV. FRANCIS WILLOUGHBY.—(1613-1671.) Services: Governor's Assistant, 1640; Member Parliament, 1658; Deputy-Governor of Massachusetts Bay Colony, 1665-1671.

REFERENCES: Colonial Records Mass. Bay Colony; General Society Year Book, 1895, p. 419.
81. George Henry Moore.
78. Joseph Edward Otis, Jr.
98. Philo Adams Otis.

SERGEANT JOHN WILSON.—[—— 1687]—Of Woburn, Mass. Soldier from June, 1675, to August, 1667. He was with Capt. Samuel Mosely in 1675, and was at Mount Hope, Aug. 9, 1675. Soldier under Capt. Richard Beers of Watertown, Mass., Jan. 25, 1676. Was under Capt. Samuel Brocklebank of Rowley, Mass. Soldier in Capt. John Cutler's Company of Charlestown, Mass., after the Sudbury disaster, King Philip's War

REFERENCE: Soldiers of King Philip's War, Bodge, pp. 21, 87, 159, 241, 315.
2. Captain Philip Reade.

SERGEANT SAMUEL WILSON.—[1658-1729]—Of Woburn, Mass., was a Corporal, 1694; Sergeant, 1695-1729, in the local military company of Militia or Train Band, being continuously in the military service from the age of 36 to 71.

REFERENCE: Savage's Genealogical Dictionary, Vol. IV, p. 588; History of Middlesex Co., p. 387; History of Woburn, p. 649.
2. Captain Philip Reade.

JOHN WINCHESTER.—(1643-1718.) Was credited with £0 9s 0d. on April 24th, 1676, for services in the Garrison at Punckapauge.

REFERENCE: Soldiers in King Philip's War, p. 364.
30. Charles Durkee Dana.
83. Alfred Henry Castle.

CAPTAIN JOHN WINCHESTER.—(1675-1751.)   Of Muddy River, was Captain of the Militia.

REFERENCE: Mass. Archives, Vol. 72, p. 117.

30.   Charles Durkee Dana.

83.   Alfred Henry Castle.

DANIEL WING—A member of the Sandwich Military Company in Plymouth Colony, August, 1643.

REFERENCE: Pierce's Colonial Lists, p. 73.

24.   Lemuel Ruggles Hall.

49.   Frank Eugene Spooner.

INCREASE WINN.—(——1690.)   Of Woburn, Mass. Served in Captain Thomas Prentice's Company in King Philip's War, 1675.

REFERENCES: Bodge's Soldiers in King's Philip's War, pp. 83 and 376; Savage's Gen. Dict., Vol. 4, p. 597.

108.   William Barker Wheelock.

LIEUTENANT EDWARD WINSHIP.—Ensign and Lieutenant, 1660; member of the Ancient and Honorable Artillery Company, 1638.

REFERENCE: Society of Colonial Wars Year Book, 1895, p. 299.

14.   Henry Sherman Boutell.

31.   Charles Newton Fessenden.

ISAAC WINSHIP.—Private in Capt. Benjamin Reed's Company of Lexington, Mass., 1759, and in Capt. Wm. Reed's Company of Lexington, Mass., in 1755.

REFERENCE: Mass. Archives, Vol. 97, p. 216; Hudson's History of Lexington, Mass., p. 378.

31.   Charles Newton Fessenden.

LIEUTENANT JOB WINSLOW.—Was in command of the Train Band at Freetown, Mass., in 1702, and served in the fight at Swansea, Mass., in 1675.

REFERENCE: Society of Colonial Wars Year Book, 1895, p. 299.

67.   John Demmon Vandercook.

JOHN WINSLOW. Of Plymouth. A member of the Plymouth Co., in August, 1643.

REFERENCE: Pierce's Colonial Lists, p. 76.

90.   Edwin Fraser Gillette.

HENRY WOLCOTT.—(1578-1655.) Chosen Assistant to the Governor, April, 1643, serving until his death.

REFERENCE: Savage, Vol. 4, p. 621.

71. Ebenezer Lane.
78. Joseph Edward Otis, Jr.
93. Wyllys King Smith.
87. Dr. Eugene Wolcott Whitney.
98. Philo Adams Otis.

HENRY WOLCOTT.—(1610-1680.) Representative, 1655-6, and 61. Assistant, 1662. Royal Charter, 1662. Member of War, 1675-6.

REFERENCE: Savage, Vol. 4, p. 621.

93. Wyllys King Smith.
87. Dr. Eugene Wolcott Whitney.

MAJOR GENERAL ROGER WOLCOTT.—[1679-1767]—Major General and second in command at siege of Louisbourg, 1745. Governor of Connecticut, 1751-1754; 1709 chosen Representative for that town in the General Assembly; 1711 went in the expedition against Canada, Commissary of the Connecticut Stores; 1714 was chosen a member of the Council; 1741 chosen Deputy Governor of this Colony; 1745 led forth the Connecticut troops on the expedition against Cape Breton and received a commission from Governor Shirley and General Law for Major General of the Army.

REFERENCE: Society of Colonial Wars Year Book, 1895, p. 300. Notes from family manuscripts in possession of Ebenezer Lane.

21. William Wolcott Strong.
71. Ebenezer Lane.

CAPTAIN SIMON WOLCOTT.—(1625-1687.) Captain of Foot at Simsbury, Conn., and Deputy, 1671 and 1675.

REFERENCES: S. C. W. 1896, p. 421; Savage's Gen. Dict., Vol. 4, p. 623.

71. Ebenezer Lane.

REV. JOHN WOODBRIDGE.—Was a member of Ancient and Honorable Military Co., Boston, 1644. Was Assistant.

REFERENCE: Savage's Gen. Dict.; Whitmore's Artillery Company; Mass. Colonial Records.

4. William Ruggles Tucker.
10. Edward Milton Adams.
24. Lemuel Ruggles Hall.

LIEUTENANT EDWARD WOODMAN.—Lieutenant, 1637; served in Pequot War.

REFERENCE: Society of Colonial Wars Year Book, p. 300.
31. Charles Newton Fessenden.

JOHN WOODS.—(——1678.) Was in October, 1675, a Sergeant of one of the Marlborough Garrison Houses.

REFERENCE: Savage's Genealogical Dictionary, Vol. 4, page 626.
1. Seymour Morris.

GEORGE WOODWARD.—Of Watertown, was private in Capt. John Cutter's Company and died while his name was still on the roll, May 31, 1676.

REFERENCE: N. E. Historical & Gen. Reg., Vol. 42, p. 299.
62. William Dorrance Messinger.

PETER WORDEN. A member of the Yarmouth, Mass., Company, under Lieut. William Palmer, in August, 1643.

REFERENCE: Pierce's Colonial Lists, p. 74.
32. James Gibson Johnson.

LIEUT. ABEL WRIGHT.—(1631-1725.) Springfield, Mass. Lieutenant.

REFERENCE: Genealogy of Lieut. Abel Wright, Springfield, Mass., from N. E. Hist. and Gen. Reg., Vol. 35, p. 74; Savage's Gen. Dict., Vol. 4, p. 684.
40. Chandler Pease Chapman.

CAPTAIN EDWARD WRIGHT.—Sudbury, Mass.; soldier in King Philip's War.

REFERENCE: Savage's Genealogical Dictionary.
25. Frank Baker.

ENSIGN JOHN WYATT.—(——1668.) Commanded a company of soldiers from Hartford in pursuit of a party of Indians, September 19th, 1677.

REFERENCES: Sheldon's Deerfield I, 182; Savage's Gen. Dict., Vol. 4, p. 661.
64. Harry Jenkins Bardwell.

JOHN WYETH.—Soldier in Capt. Gookin's Company, King Philip's War.

REFERENCE: Year Book General Society of Colonial Wars, 1895, p. 300.
31. Charles Newton Fessenden.

GOVERNOR GEORGE WYLLYS. Deputy Governor, 1641, and Governor of Connecticut, in 1642.

REFERENCES: N. E. H. & G. R., Vol. 37, pp. 33 and 37; Savage's Gen. Dictionary, Vol. 4, p. 574.

101. John Newbury Bagley.

FRANCIS WYMAN. Served under Captain Thomas Prentice in the Mount Hope Campaign, and was credited on August 27th, 1675, with £2, 1s, 6d, and on March 24th, 1675-6, he was credited with £4, 10s, for services.

REFERENCE: Bodge's Soldiers in King Philip's War, pp. 81 and 83.

107. Charles David Mill.

JOHN WYMAN.—Member of Capt. Prentiss' Company of 73 troopers in Middlefield. "A list of Major Sam. Appleton souldiers yt were slaine & wounded the 19th Decemb 75 at the Indians' fort at Narragansett; of Captaine Prentise his troopers slaine & wounded Jno. Wyman slaine."

REFERENCE: Massachusetts Archives, Vol. 68, p. 73; Vol. 68, p. 104.

22. Walter Channing Wyman.

LIEUTENANT JOHN WYMAN.—Lieutenant in Captain Thomas Prentiss' Company; fought at Mount Hope and the Narragansett campaign, and at last received a wound in the face. Registered in Capt. Prentiss' troops Aug. 27, 1675, to June 24, 1676.

REFERENCE: Massachusetts Archives, Vol. 68, p. 104; New England Historical & Genealogical Register, pp. 280, 281, 282.

22. Walter Channing Wyman.